Tipton Poetry J

Editor's Note

Tipton Poetry Journal, located in the heartland of the Midwest, publishes quality poetry from Indiana and around the world.

This issue features 49 poets from the United States (24 different states) and 10 poets from Australia, Bangladesh, Canada, Germany, Ireland, Japan, the Philippines, and Switzerland.

Cover Photo: "Eel River Bridge" by Barry Harris

Print versions of *Tipton Poetry Journal* are available for purchase through <u>amazon.com</u>.

Barry Harris, Editor
Riley Childers, Assistant Editor

Tipton Poetry Journal is published by Brick Street Poetry Inc., a tax-exempt non-profit organization under IRS Code 501(c)(3). Brick Street Poetry Inc. publishes the Tipton Poetry Journal, hosts the monthly poetry series *Poetry on Brick Street* and sponsors other poetry-related events.

Contents

Lucky Duck

Roger Camp

It's a four by six intersection,
twenty-four lanes in all,
wrangling among themselves
to continue.
No matter. The mallard majorette,
ignoring all signals
and streaming traffic
has set her course,
marching her band of babies
to the beat
of her own drum.
Behind the windshield
eyes shut
I strain for sounds
of demise. No thunk
of duck breast on metal,
no dust devil of feathers,
no Greek chorus.
Making evolutionary tracks
a revolutionary hen
and her dozen ducklings
make their escape.

Roger Camp lives in Seal Beach, California where he
gardens, walks the pier, plays blues piano and spends
afternoons with his pal, Harry, over drinks at Nick's on 2nd.
When he's not at home, he's traveling in the Old World. His
work has appeared in *Pank*, *Southern Poetry Review* and
Nimrod.

Our Crypt
Dick Bentley

Nothing will sleep in our basement,
It's damp as a ditch,
Small flowers break out of boxes stalking
cracks in the concrete.
Buds swayed and slouched,
Dangling from moldy crates,
Drooped down long yellow vile stalks, like serpents.
And what a muster of stinks!
Roots with wet shafts,
muck, green, swollen against slimy planks.
Striving for life:
While the muck keeps gasping.

Under the Weather — A Funeral
Dick Bentley

Damp church pews glistened with
grief. Sorrow poured out and rushed freely
from our eyes.
Our pain came
as if from a hidden song in the bible.

We suffered, knelt, pleaded, chanted,
compromised with God while asking
for words of certainty.

We blasphemed, sought assurance, we mourners in black,
full of holy struggle, our hands and faces damp,
from the edges of understanding.

Dick Bentley's books, *Post-Freudian Dreaming, A General Theory of Desire, and All Rise* are available on Amazon. He won the Paris Writers/Paris Review's International Fiction Award and has published over 280 works of fiction, poetry, and memoir in the US, the UK, France, Canada, and Brazil. He served on the Board of the Modern Poetry Association and has taught at the University of Massachusetts. Find him online at www.dickbentley.com.

Syncopated Time

Yvonne

Time was breathing softly, slowly
One...and...two...and Hollywood horns
Burst their cage
With a toothy chanteuse riding riding
All Aboard! Swirling up the ceiling
Across the floor out the door down the — OFF!
And the melody slithered back
Behind the grille
Of a shrimp-colored plastic radio clock,
Mid-century modern sleek.

In those days
Mother was my alarm
"Get up! Get up! You'll be late for school!"
So my first radio,
A cute turquoise jewel of a box,
Had no clock.
I set it near the dangerous edge
Of my night stand
Long after lights out, way down low
Ella bopped tippily jippily wah-de-woo!

When it fell, smashed, not saved
By its electric cord,
My fourteenth year brought me
A portable powered
By a bulky battery
To carry to the summer park
Like a proper white pocketbook,
Baby sister toddling along
As safety guard. Didn't my midnight
Pillow muffle the rock/roll, roll/rock?

Deeper into the 'Sixties, drunk with college
Philosophy (a little beer?),

I turned to late night airwave talk,
Bitter, wry and wary;
The bright plastic radio box
Had morphed into black and brown
Nap and metal—just like the driven
Surge and beat. The lucky clangor
Of a mini Big Ben
Stopped my eleventh-hour snore.

I've been a hoot owl
Forced to sing in the key
Of the lark
For forty-plus years
Whether 9 to 5 or 8 to 4—Now,
My days are without such borders.
None of my clocks are Yanks.
Never were they Swiss.
Alarms don't work for me—
Eating my corn flakes at noon!

Yvonne (aka Yvonne Chism-Peace) is the first poetry editor of two pioneer feminist magazines, *Aphra* and *Ms.* She has received several awards including two NEAs for poetry and a Leeway for fiction. Anthologies and annuals featuring her poems include: *Bryant Literary Review, Pinyon, Nassau Review 2019, Bosque Press #8, Foreign Literary Journal #1, Quiet Diamonds 2018, 161 One-Minute Monologues from Literature, This Sporting Life, Bless Me, Father: Stories of Catholic Childhood, Catholic Girls, Tangled Vines, Celebrations: A New Anthology of Black American Poetry, Pushcart Prize Anthology,* and *We Become New.* Yvonne lives in Philadelphia.

2020

CL Bledsoe

Weren't there worse times
than this? My father side-eyed
a world war that claimed his
brother, drank his way across
Japan. My uncle was on the wrong
side of history in Little Rock, stood
over a mountain of Korean skulls
in a photo Mamaw hid in the attic,
but they assured us Jesus forgave
him on his deathbed. These
are just the horrors I know. Ancient
tree limbs grooved. Bodies kept
from the river. Time isn't so much
a cycle as a wheel, grinding
to a stop. Once it shakes us off,
it will probably roll smoother.

CL Bledsoe's most recent poetry collection is *Trashcans in Love*. He lives in northern Virginia with his daughter, and blogs, with Michael Gushue, at
https://medium.com/@howtoeven

Contemplating Dead Poets at Crown Hill Cemetery

Gabriele Glang

Standing on the cemetery's summit
in the shade of imposing faux-Greek
columns – James Riley's memorial,
a majestic temple that defies
forgetting – I think: *Here's a city*
that reveres its poets. But we can't
find the black poet's last resting place,
although we drive around this mammoth
place of remembrance twice. So I ask
for intervention: *Etheridge Knight,*
send us a sign to help us find you!

We've given up, pausing at the gates,
discussing where to have our lunch,
when a man appears – familiar, friend,
poet, and pallbearer of the ghost
we sought: Michaal Collins is the flesh-
and-blood proof Etheridge's spirit
heard my plea. Embroidering his talk
with poetry, his own and others',
Michaal takes us to the simple stone
inscribed *POET SON FATHER BROTHER*
WE FREE SINGERS BE. I get it now.

Woven in our DNA, this need
to part our lips and sing. Poetry
was the beginning. A lullaby
of vowels crooned to soothe the sleepless.
Prayer. Incantation to the sun,
that it may rise again tomorrow.
As long as there are songs to sing
and ears to hear, poetry will be
beneath our soles, within us, airborne –
a ballet of winged words spiraling
in air like starlings' murmurations.

Gabriele Glang, is a German-American bilingual poet and artist. Gabriele Glang has been living in a small village on the Swabian Alb in southern Germany for nearly three decades. In 2017 Klöpfer & Meyer Verlag published her German poetry debut, *Göttertage*, fictional monologues of German Expressionist painter Paula Modersohn-Becker. A screenwriter and freelance translator in the film sector, Glang teaches creative writing in English at the University of Applied Sciences at Esslingen. www.gabrieleglang.de.

Successfully Grieving
Charles Grosel

I no longer think of your soft
voice reading *Go, Dog. Go!*
in the slant of the afternoon sun,
our legs tickled by the prickly
beige couch, me pleading more,
read more, to which you oblige
until the shadows crawl in and
the arm not pressed against
the warmth of your leg bristles
at the oncoming chill. You say
it's time to get dinner, leaving me
shivery and alone, just as I am
this damp morning successfully
grieving the day you died.

What a Poem Can Do

Charles Grosel

you can use a poem
to light the pilot
when the gas goes out

poems stacked thick enough
take the wobble from a chair,
slide back a door latch

you can use a poem
to cut cocaine, to count
your pills, to roll your pot

between the lines of a poem
you can draw up a million dollar
scheme or a grocery list

a poem can line the
bottom of a birdcage,
house train a puppy

you can fan yourself
when it's hot, and line your
shoes when it's cold

the hard corner of a poem
cleans the dirt
from under your nails

a poem is a bumper
sticker, a pennant flying
at a funeral

you can stuff a poem

in the back of a picture frame
to hold the memory fast

you can roll up a poem,
stick it in a toaster,
incinerate the past

when you cut a poem
into a jigsaw, you
make it new

a poem is a dream catcher,
a spell book, a mind map,
a book of days

you can wave goodbye
with a poem,
or whisper in her ear

and you just might woo
beauty to bed, part her pale
folds, sing her into rapture

Tourist Deck at Dawn

Charles Grosel

The sun moons above the Canyon's rim,
burns away the dawn fog, the smell of night must.
The sun ascends and stings my eyes open.
I'm standing on the tourist deck, sinuses hard
and full, tingling with the pine sap conveyed
on the mist. A bighorn alights on the cliff,
blood quickens: a ram, horns spiraling
like the river's eddies, like masks of pagan gods.

The ram spurns the path winding smoothly
from the Canyon floor, picks its own way
up the cliff face, step by steady step.
O sheep, ledged the width of a pebble,
it must be divine levitation holds you
where humans scramble and fall. I stand safe
above you, hands tight on the cold rail.
O ram whose coiled haunches ripple
like a valley of grass, like a flag in the wind,
like the sheet of my traveling companion
still humming her dream song in the scent
of our rut, fly to me now like the dart
of a practiced hand, the bolt of a crossbow,
the lethal shower of a catapult, soar to me
like a kite burning its tether through our hands,
a rocket hissing across the sky.

Carve me up like the river that plowed this
canyon from dry earth, the quilted, bruised valley
peeled away by the sun. Fly to me, enter me,
give me your power, your calm agility,
your submission to what is. I stand
on the tourist deck, trembling in the mist,
voice my desire to the Canyon, which resounds
with a grammar of its own: deep, deeper, deepest.

The Return of the Warrior Queen
Charles Grosel

The longboat knocks
Against the splintered dock,
Oars cocked. You'd never think
The still, silent woman
In the charcoal cloak
Was the cause of such mustering
But for the coil of bronze
Sprung from her hood, and that
All eyes are on her.
The black-robed council
Shifts from foot to foot—
They have their own journey
Ahead. But for just this one
Last moment she lets herself
Think how the boat's beat
Is like that of the birdfeeder
Swinging from her cottage eaves
And how the songbirds
Are the first to flee
The dogs of war.
She throws back the cowl,
Her jumbled mane now
Ablaze in the moon,
And waves off the soldier
Extending his hand.
When she steps onto the plank,
Her legions make ready to march.

An editor, writer, and poet, **Charles Grosel** lives in Arizona. He has published stories in *Western Humanities Review, Red Cedar Review, Water-Stone,* and *The MacGuffin* as well as poems in *Tipton Poetry Review, Slate, The Threepenny Review, Poet Lore,* and *Harpur Palate,* among others. To pay the bills, Charles owns the communications firm, *Write for Success.*

Get Real

Dave Seter

In my nightmare Ice Cream Truck No. 1
rocking *Pop Goes the Weasel*
veers left and if this were slapstick
the script might read collision with

Ice Cream Truck No.2 out of shot
with rolling hubcaps and tearing metal.
Life is dangerous, my doctor tells me
as he reads out my sugar and cholesterol.

I plead with him to *let me eat just one*
electric blue snow-cone, but
in his white coat he wags his finger: *no.*
He's forgotten what it means to be a child.

In my nightmare behind the mulberry bush
neighbors take up the chant for frozen treats.
Please, they are hungry. Like me they want
to chase the weasel of the ice cream truck.

No ice cream, my doctor prescribes,
and denies my inner child. But listen to p
the chorus of kids outside—I say—get real—
they say—their rainbow faces singing.

Dave Seter is a civil engineer and poet. Originally from Chicago, he currently lives in Sonoma County, California. His poetry and critical works have recently appeared in *Paterson Literary Review, Evansville Review, Palaver, Confluence,* and other journals. He received his undergraduate degree from Princeton University and his graduate degree from Dominican University of California, where he studied ecopoetics. His poetry chapbook *Night Duty* was published in 2010 by *Main Street Rag Publishing Company.*

Take Me Too

Carl "Papa" Palmer

I speak her name.
She returns with a start
from where she'd been.

I clasp her hands,
find them cold,
hold until warm.

She turns her head,
gazes past my shoulder
at nothing I can see.

She's going back
to where she'd been.
I want to come along.

Vacancy

Carl "Papa" Palmer

curtains closed clock shows 4 AM or PM
seated heavily at my kitchen table
gripping a cup of twice heated cold coffee
still in pajamas busy being alone
in this space once ours gathering stillness

rereading the page of unwritten words
sought then forgotten pencil poised
awaiting a first line for this poem

Carl "Papa" Palmer of Old Mill Road in
Ridgeway, Virginia, lives in University Place,
Washington. He is retired from the military and
Federal Aviation Administration (FAA) enjoying life
now as "Papa" to his grand descendants and being a
Franciscan Hospice volunteer. Carl is a *Pushcart
Prize* and *Micro Award* nominee.

13

The Hermit

Donald Gasperson

a hermit
desireless one

I maybe
empty inside

the one who
apologizes

to every nut
in the square

frigid
or frightened

the market
calculates the cost

of my
disease

with a view
to my dishabille

prescribes
expediency

and
loneliness

Donald Gasperson earned a Bachelor of Science degree in Psychology and a Master of Arts degree in Clinical Psychology working as a psychiatric rehabilitation counselor. After a lifetime of reading taking another step to writing was natural and self-affirming. Recognizing art in the insight at our fingertips was absorbing. He has had poetry published in *Quail Bell Magazine, The Bitchn" Kitsch, Big Windows Review, Foliate Oak Literary Review, Better Than Starbucks* and *Tipton Poetry Journal* among others. He lives in Klamath Falls, Oregon.

Home
Leah Stenson

More ephemeral than a dream,
a touchstone of the heart,
an invisible locus
in the recess of memory
where one returns
for connection,
a creation of one's own,
a heaven or hell.

Leah Stenson lives in Oregon and is the author of two
chapbooks, *Heavenly Body* and *The Turquoise Bee and Other
Love Poems* (Finishing Line Press: 2011 and 2014, respectively); a
regional editor of *Alive at the Center: Contemporary Poems from
the Pacific Northwest* (Ooligan Press, 2013) and co-editor of
Reverberations from Fukushima (Inkwater Press, 2014) which
was awarded finalist status in the category of Social Change in the
USA Best Book Awards and first place for Poetry in the Pacific Rim
Book Festival.. Her full-length book of poetry *Everywhere I Find
Myself* was published by Turning Point in December 2017. She
serves on the board of Tavern Books. Please see
www.leahstenson.com.

A Recipe for Slick Dumplings
Gayle Compton

Eva May, honey
I just had to call and let you know
they finally found my
ex-husband John B.

Been a-missing
ever since he started working for
the government somers around Houston.

Been two years this September
but they finally found him—
found all of him but his head.

You heard me right!
Said he was chopped up and scattered
fours ways to Sunday.
Arm here, leg yonder—
but nary a head.

They said it didn't take the coroner
mor'en thirty minutes
to pronounce him dead.
Eva May,

do you still have Mommy's old recipe
for slick dumplings?

I've racked my brain
trying to remember
if it takes three pound of chicken
or four,
whether to let'em simmer
or bring 'em to a bile.

Gayle Compton writes about the most interesting and most misunderstood people in America, the common people of Eastern Kentucky--his people, from the hard-working to the bare-assed and proud. With a background in teaching and broadcasting he has been published in numerous journals and anthologies, including *Main Street Rag, Blue Mountain Review, U.S. 1 Worksheets,* and *Tipton Poetry Journal.* Gayle lives with his wife Sharon at Jonancy, Kentucky, the "Peabrook" setting for much of his work.

Writer's Block

Steve Klepetar

It's not Writer's Block, that imaginary disease,
but Writer's Sloth that grips me now,
especially in spring, such a hard season
for an indolent man. Snow recedes, reveals
in its wet wake detritus on the lawn –
old leaves and broken sticks, bits of shingles
that blew off the roof in a winter windstorm,
so much muck to rake and haul. Who can write?
Deck furniture needs scrubbing, the grill,
left filthy for months, cries out for cleaning.
It's early yet, but I can see trees threatening
to leaf out. There's a faint green glow
on the mountains and a few robins hopping
in the yard. I should do the wash, clean the tub,
get the garbage out to the curb.
Magazines piling up on the rack, kids to watch,
hair to get cut, clothes to give away.
But now they say a blizzard's moving in,
maybe two feet of snow to close down everything,
white and silent, answer to the prayers of a lazy man.

The Hole of Forgotten Names

Steve Klepetar

Here is the deep place, the Hole of Forgotten Names.
Here is the burial ground, place of ghosts and wind.
What have you whispered here behind tombstones
and cypress trees? What hymns have you sung
to forgotten gods? Here are your grandmothers' names,
Herta and Theresa, the names of your aunts
who followed the black river down: Claudia and Rose,
Vivian and Bertha and Martha and Blanche.
They rode on the backs of swans as water swirled
around their heavy limbs. They would have loved you,
even with your strange tongue and wild hair.
They would have given you the gift of their old ways,
their wrinkled hands, their hair tied back and their talk
of a country bathed in mist. They would have held you
in their arms, laughed in sunlight as you gazed at them,
strange old ladies in the park. They would have watched
you grow away in your long strides, playing games
they never knew. They would have watched, waiting
on flimsy chairs. They would have sat at the corner
with dark eyes aflame if only they had survived,
if only their bones had not been ground to ash and dust

Steve Klepetar lives in the Berkshires in
Massachusetts. His work has received several
nominations for Best of the Net and the Pushcart Prize.
The most recent of his fourteen collections include *A
Landscape in Hell, Why Glass Shatters*, and *The Coffee
Drinker's Son*.

The Delta Blues

Katherine Cottle

The land, they say
goes down farther than anywhere else,
twice the length of a grown man,
deeper than a river,
or at least some part of the river,
where a child could easily drown
without knowing how to swim.

The land, they say
is so fertile, it cannot let go of
its long rows of crops:
cotton, soybean, corn, rice--
never-ending paths to the sun
that meet the horizon, that lead one away
from the road, even without trying.

The land, they say
was once covered with trees,
a hardwood forest,
an alluvial floodplain,
a place almost too impenetrable to find.
It took years to clear.
It took money to develop; lives to support.

The land, they say
produced the sounds, the rhythms.
The cotton fields gave birth to the voices,
the instruments, the music;
the rows grew skin, muscle, blood,
the roots, leaves, and bolls
of love and loss, chopped and picked.

The land, they say.

They say: The land.
They land and learn a new way to say
what they feel, what they know
of this place, soaked with a past
that goes down farther and wider
and deeper than even its own river.

Katherine Cottle is a past contributor of the *Tipton Poetry Journal* and author of four full-length books--*The Hidden Heart of Charm City (forthcoming October 2019)*, *I Remain Yours (2014)*, *Halfway (2010)*, and *My Father's Speech (2008)*, all published by Apprentice House/Loyola University Maryland. More information can be found at www.katherinecottle.com

Stroke

Sean Kelbley

Tap-tap-tap, and then
a sudden opening—as if a child
with a hammer and a child's curiosity
found bullets in a secret drawer inside
my head. It's true about the

Light, except it feels like
insomnia. Is my tuition paid?
Did we ever sell that rotting house?
A tunnel fades into an ocean,
quiet as distant wings.
No wonder people go.

I'll say I had the choice—
if I remember. But it's the tiny
moon of you, the shiny crescent
of your shoe, that grabs the tide.
Reverses it. Re-dresses me

in scales I've shed for you
(how many times?)
like skin.

Sean Kelbley lives on a farm in southeastern Ohio, in a house he and his husband
built. He works as an elementary school counselor. Sean's poetry has been
recognized in contests at *Midwest Review, Still: The Journal, Up North Lit, the Yuki
Teikei Haiku Society*, and has appeared online and/or in print at *Crab Creek
Review, One, Rattle, Rise Up Review* (2017 Best of the Net nomination), and other
wonderful places.

Cool Spirit

Keith Moul

This prodigious plain scars us to life hereafter,
imprisons our spirits to homestead as if hasped
in forced place while rasped inside a hurricane.

My mother made of this rivulet her preferred
place to recuperate her will and her emotions
within these spinning forces and her gravity.

She taught me special things about flat lands:
demanding, not dull; requiring powerful work;
early need to survive, constantly to recover.

She came here each spring, one or more days,
her feet dangling in the cool water, her mind
thwarting summer after blood washes storm.

Keith Moul has written poems and taken
photos for more than 50 years, his work
appearing in magazines widely. His chapbook,
The Journal, was recently accepted by Duck
Lake Chaps for issuance in early 2020. This is
his ninth chap or book published. These
poems follow the voices of pioneers over wide
plains of the U.S. Keith Moul has lived among
these voices, owes them fealty because people
survive the plains under the most adverse
conditions. He has come to appreciate the knack to this bravery, now much later in
his life.

Playing with the Bulls

Marne Wilson

After the calves followed their mothers to the pasture,
I looked for some new friends.
Nobody ever learned that after school,
before surrendering my freedom
by crossing the threshold of the house,
I stole away to visit the yearling bulls.

I knew my parents wouldn't approve,
but I was certain the bulls could never hurt me.
Not only had they been my playmates the year before,
but I was also aware of my female power,
knew I could use it to charm the unsuspecting
and soothe the savage breast.

On tiptoe, I reached my hands confidently over the gate.
The young bulls were like big friendly dogs,
jostling roughly for my touch,
sometimes licking me with their sandpapery tongues.
Although it hurt, I knew it was worth it
to be the focus of attention for a moment.

[Originally appeared in *The Bovine Daycare Center*, Finishing Line Press, 2015]

The Juicer

Marne Wilson

My sister used to make me fresh squeezed juice,
selecting the perfect orange from the red string bag,
slicing it open without spilling a drop,
then twisting it back and forth around
the battle-scarred cone of the juicer
until there was nothing left but a casing.

It always felt like a waste to use so many oranges
to make one small glass of juice,
but they don't keep well at room temperature.
Leave them sitting too long in the fruit bowl,
and they'll grow soft, then moldy.

So often I treat people the same way my sister treated oranges.
Instead of taking my time
to peel back the layers and separate the sections,
I favor the quick and violent approach,
taking up with one new person at a time
and pressing out as much goodness as I can possibly get.

Then again, the kind of people I usually choose
are as ephemeral as a ripe orange in ninety degree weather.
They can't last long anyway, so
I need to take my drink of summer sweetness
before they go.

[Originally appeared in *The Bovine Daycare Center*, Finishing Line Press, 2015]

The Traveler

Marne Wilson

She never told us she was leaving.
She just sauntered down the road one autumn day
without ever stopping to look back.
We often say that barn cats are wanderers,
owing allegiance to no one
and going wherever the wind blows them,
but what we really mean by that is "tomcats."
Just as with humans, females are expected
to uphold a higher standard of reliability.
Good girls don't go wandering.

But all the same, Spitzy did leave that day,
which told my parents she had gone forever.
(When women finally do leave,
it is always final.)
All that winter, I waited like a forlorn suitor,
gazing out my bedroom window each day
hoping to discover her hiding somewhere in the yard.

Even so, I was surprised to awaken one spring morning
and see her sitting serenely by the barn door
as if she had never gone.
Not stopping to get dressed, I ran outside and greeted her.
She seemed no worse for wear, still the same old Spitzy.
I learned from this that faith is sometimes rewarded,
but also that a good girl can still be free.

[Originally appeared in *The Bovine Daycare Center*, Finishing Line Press, 2015]

The Fruitcake Charm

Marne Wilson

As a girl, I sought after love magic,
testing every incantation and old wives' tale
that promised to foretell future bliss.
I tossed orange peels over my shoulder,
counted every button on my blouse,
and rotated each apple stem until it broke off.
Once, I even ate a cake of ashes
to see my future husband's face in a dream.

Despite my best efforts,
none of these spells worked,
so when I declared
that any man who tasted my fruitcake
would love me forever,
it seemed like another silly game.
The only boy who ever tried it was
a gormless neighbor.
If he loved me, he never said,
so it did me no good.

But when I found you
and longed to keep you for all time,
although I felt too old for such hokum,
I bought myself some brand new fruitcake pans.
I couldn't find my old and faithful recipe,
so I chose one at random from the cookbook.
It was a complete and total disaster.

The next December I found my old recipe,
right where it should have been all along,
and I made it for a new man
who has been mine ever since.

So now the question I ask myself is this:
did I lose you because of a bad fruitcake,
or did the fruitcake refuse to bless our union?

[Originally appeared in *As Lovers Always Do*, Etchings Press, 2019]

Marne Wilson lives in Parkersburg, West Virginia. Her poems have recently appeared in *Whale Road Review* and *Hobart* and are forthcoming in *Gargoyle* and *Crab Orchard Review*. She is the author of two chapbooks, *The Bovine Daycare Center (Finishing Line, 2015)* and *As Lovers Always Do (Etchings Press, 2019)*.

Above the Fire
Joe Albanese

Above the fire is
where every phrase gets
coined. Just like the spider
walks that
careful line, we are just a
momentary lapse
from miracle or disaster.
Call me a coward
and I'll call you a fool.
This is where I make my
home; this is where life
is won or lost.

Joe Albanese is a writer from South Jersey. His fiction, nonfiction, and poetry can be found in publications across the U.S. and in ten other countries. Joe is the author of *Smash and Grab, Caina, For the Blood is the Life, Candy Apple Red,* and a poetry collection, *Cocktails with a Dead Man*.

Royalty

Roger Pfingston

Upside down, her white
  rump veiled by sun-
shot dust, Dinalda,
   Arabian princess, rolls

barn free in the pleasure
  of a June pasture, gold
clouds floating wet
   in eyes the size of plums.

Risen, she seems to bow
  when she lowers her head
to the evening grass,
   the geese in the pond,

the air above a bee-
  line hum of workers
laden with half their weight
   returning to the queen.

Full Circle

Roger Pfingston

Faint hum of bumblebees,
heavy in the honeysuckle,
when something tears out
of that sweet mass,

a thrashing that gives him
pause before he takes
the path again, head
aslant, ear cocked, half

amused by his wary mind
(fitful solitude even here),
thinking it must be close
to full circle, the trail he chose,

his the only car in the lot
on a Sunday morning fraught
with heat, the lake's glazed
silence rippled by distant bells.

Roger Pfingston is the recipient of two PEN Syndicated Fiction
Awards and a poetry fellowship from the National Endowment for
the Arts. He lives in Bloomington, Indiana and is the author of
Something Iridescent, a collection of poetry and fiction, as well as
four chapbooks: *Earthbound, Singing to the Garden,* and *A Day
Marked for Telling* and *What's Given*. He has poems in *I-70
Review, U.S. 1 Worksheets, Plainsongs, Innisfree Poetry Journal,
American Journal of Poetry,* and *Poet Lore*.

Poems at her Doorstep

John Tustin

I leave my poems at her doorstep,
Hunching in the rain
And scurrying away before she sees me -

Not knowing that in spite of the light
Coming out through her bedroom window
She is not home
But somewhere else, with someone else
Who will try to tell her how he feels
In some other way than words affixed to a page

But she will return home and,
Upon finding the soggy pages at her feet
She will scoop them up and rescue them
Into the tidy dryness of her kitchen

Where she will spread out the pages on the table
And read them, one at a time
While thinking about me
And thinking about her,
The ink running a little
Onto her hands
And into
Her heart.

John Tustin began writing poetry after in February 2008 after a ten year hiatus and finally became brave enough to submit to magazines in April of 2009. In August of that year received his first acceptance from Poem and from *Straylight* that December. Since then his poetry has appeared in well over 100 literary journals, online and in print. fritzware.com/johntustinpoetry contains links to his published poetry online.

Behind A Miracle

Rehanul Hoque

Taking a shower in the orange coloured sunshine your body is now
A miracle on earth.

In utter darkness with all hopes gone, your eyes bright as lighthouse
Keep dreams evergreen in a secluded island
Your eyebrows sharp as curved swords are the fomenting force
of unrestrained *Vaisakha*- fuelled by revolting sensation.
Your jelly-filled arms encourage hailing drudgery of life as sweet memories
Your lips as ruddy as ruby store the terrible pull of gravity
And spanning across the hadal zone with low temperature, optimum pressure
each of your breaths create wonder around you - you, the sole inmate.

Time is wonderstruck by your navel, the hourglass
goes on wooing to fall in everlasting love
The juncture of your thighs, in fact, the mouth of the volcano
Omnivorous, albeit allurement of happiness all through.
Your radiant cells are numberless kingdoms of diversity
Your veins are replete with unbounded flows of love,
whirling around you.

Your joint steps are indicators of civilization
Your expression, the fundament of sensation and
Your wrath is another name of complete annihilation.

Undoubtedly, your suitors are too many
In the fight for love, I am bound to surrender to your desire
I know someone else rules your heart
Yet, it is only you that I am destined to love.

Rehanul Hoque, born in the village of Majkhuria in Bangladesh, studied M.A in
English literature and pursued an MSc in International Development from a UK
University. He is a bilingual poet and started writing poems at an early age. Though
he has an interest in different forms of literature, his first and foremost love
is **p**oetry. Rehanul lives in Bangladesh.

Highland Café

Stephen Campiglio

Playing in my hedgerow hide-out
on a workday afternoon,
I spy on the beer truck
that stops in front of the bar
next door to my grandparent's house.

He watches two young men restock kegs
through an opened cellar grating
for the old men, taking their turn inside.

A foreign odor from below
reaches up to the sidewalk
and over to my nose.

The stale smoke-and-booze smell
of this adult playground intrigues him so.

Years later, I'd be one of the old men inside,
drinking through workday afternoons.

Stephen Campiglio's poems and translations have recently appeared or are forthcoming in *Aji Magazine, Chiron Review, City Works Journal, Journal of Italian Translation, Manzano Mountain Review, Miramar, TAB: The Journal of Poetry & Poetics,* and *Tipton Poetry Journal.* His new translation project is focused on the work of Italian poet, Giovanni Pascoli (1855-1912). A quarterfinalist in the 2018 Codhill Press poetry contest for a book-length manuscript and nominated for two Pushcart Prizes, Campiglio has published two chapbooks, *Cross-Fluence (2012)* and *Verbal Clouds through Various Magritte Skies (2014).*

Do Not Dispose

Karla Linn Merrifield

It's only a turquoise cocktail paper napkin,
albeit embossed in silver, Hollybrook House,
bracketed by wispy swirls, custom-ordered
in a rare Martha Stewart indulgence
to celebrate my celebrated home, sweet, home.

It was used only once, barely a crinkle
in it, a few cookie crumbs yet on it,
and, I reckon, marking it, traces of DNA
from the lips of the man who also
left his famous grin impressed upon it.

It's only a fancy-schmancy napkin, heaven's sake,
but you'll find this extraordinarily ordinary
(if pricey) artifact of first desires—paper thin—
saved between the pages of this book;
see August 8, 2018; how fragile, posterity.

Mecca

Karla Linn Merrifield

Riding the Long Island Railroad eastward,
I clickety-clack past Whitman's house;
wheels squeal to a stop at the nearest station
to the boyhood abode where Heyen once resided;
but I stay aboard; I rock: I sway, almost
to the end of the poetic line to detrain
in little known East Moriches to enter
the inhabited rooms of a "lesser poet"—
says who?—who is now mapping
my imagination as Walt, as Bill, have done,
word by word, line by line, in long Time.

I want to lightly fingertip
his dirty dishes in the sink
and stacks of manuscript pages;
trip over books, journals, the shirt he wore the night before;
press my face into his bath towels
and his bedsheets;
and kneel on his bare floor,
because *he* sleeps here.

Villanelle of the *Queen Mary 2*
Karla Lynn Merrifield

O, to sail like an ocean liner plying the sea,
every nautical mile to accept Poseidon's moist kiss.
Steady, steady on toward near infinity.

O, to set a soul-changing course by star's mythologies,
wave-chasing Orion's constellated bliss.
O, to sail like an ocean liner plying the sea,

O, to navigate in moon's tidal grip of ebb and neap,
to consort with Hecate in a benthic tryst.
Steady, steady on toward near infinity.

O, to cavort in gyre within the watery
realms of behemoths and hear their spoutings' hiss.
O, to sail like an ocean liner plying the sea.

O, to be foam, spindrift, the wind itself—free,
aloft in an Aeolian embrace above the blue abyss.
Steady, steady on toward near infinity.

O, to be a woman on a storied ship voyaging nearly endlessly.
O, then to come alongside, make fast, reminisce.
O, to sail like an ocean liner plying the sea.
Steady, steady on toward near infinity.

Karla Lynn Merrifield, a nine-time Pushcart Prize nominee and National Park Artist-in-Residence, has had 700+ poems appear in dozens of journals and anthologies. She has 14 books to her credit. Following her 2018 *Psyche's Scroll* (Poetry Box Select) is the newly released full-length book *Athabaskan Fractal: Poems of the Far North from Cirque Press. Her Godwit: Poems of Canada* (FootHills Publishing) received the Eiseman Award for Poetry. She now lives in Florida and is a frequent contributor to *The Songs of Eretz Poetry Review*, and assistant editor and poetry book reviewer Emerita for *The Centrifugal Eye*.

White Papered Steaks

Joseph Buehler

I watched as distant flat fields and tall trees
slowly darkened into a Saturday evening. We
were in a painted-white wooden framed restaurant
back in nineteen fifty six at the edge of a southern
Michigan town called Vicksburg. Elvis was on
television in black and white up in a corner. Gyrating.
He was a sensation, of course.

My mother and I dined on now long forgotten specials.
My mother was somewhat overweight. She had a broad
nose and blonde hair and large blue eyes and, in the winter,
she usually wore a cheap black coat that didn't look like it
would keep her warm enough. She also usually wore a
small unstylish black hat. She was very careful about money
because she had to be.

When we were in town, my stepfather would play cards with
his friends at a bar. Frozen white papered steaks, hamburgers
and roasts were being kept for us in a local freezer in the town.
We would select some of them later to carry home to our farm
 which was situated about twelve miles away.

I escaped a year later after my high school graduation. I left in
the summer to go and live with my father and his wife and my
step-sister in urban Ohio. Our house there was positioned up on
a fashionable hillside; it was a two storied white house with dark
green trim. It had a very steep backyard.

My father sold Swiss cheese to bars and grocery stores from a
new model (he traded every other year) black Chevrolet panel
truck. Sometimes I helped him. "This is my *boy!*" he would
boast proudly to his customers.

Joseph Buehler has published 98 poems in *Nine Mile Magazine, Sentinel Literary Quarterly (U.K.), Ottawa Arts Review, Indiana Voice Journal, Otoliths (Australia), The Tower Journal, The Opiate, H.C.E. Review (Dublin), Angry Old Man Magazine, Common Ground Review, Blue Bonnet Review,* and others.. He is retired and lives in Georgia with his wife Trish. He was a finalist for the *Adelaide Literary Award in poetry (NYC)* in February and October 2018.

Going Through

Thomas Osatchoff

The gates
at the top
staircase.
Trauma
remembering itself.
Trauma remembering who we are?
In case
we never really went extinct.
Any form we want.
Any day—one of these days.
Different names
doesn't mean actual difference.
We can't handle the truth but we can handle these lies?
What do lies sound like when they fall down the stairs?

Thomas Osatchoff, together with family, is
building a self-sustaining home near a waterfall
in The Philippines. Recent poems have appeared
in *Breakwater Review, FOLIO, HCE Review*,
and elsewhere.

Once and for All

Timothy Robbins

Once and only once I drew
a picture of a laughing kid.
My recollection of its origin
is coy, hinting it was
inspired by a remark of my
father's or an acute urge to
placate him. Shortly after

its making, it disappeared.

Not like it was stolen or
mislaid or given to a boy-
friend who kept it when
we broke up. Rather, like
a dream that waking erases.
This morning, browsing

through canvases in the
closet (the motion of flip-
ping through albums at the
Goodwill Store) I was
alarmed by my expertise
with scowling faces. Dizzy,
I looked up and there on the

blank wall: his pale green
sweater with braided collar,
his mouth like the end of
a very small megaphone,
his toy-like teeth, his large
brown head thrown back,
filling the frame.

Ending

Timothy Robbins

What I brought you the
first night in our second
home — and years later
when we'd decided to
move again — and to
adopt, at last,
Kit and Caboodle,
the cats of our dreams —
was an urge you hadn't
felt since they wrenched
you from Hanoi and a
coverless *Thorn Birds* at
the age of nine.

"My fingers remember,"
you said both times.
What you gave me was
a transformation of
typing paper to canoe
and swan. How many
crises since have loaded
that boat? How many
times has the swan
pulled it to safe harbor?
How handsome I'll
rest when I lie at last
in this sturdy vessel.

Timothy Robbins has been teaching English as a Second
Language for 28 years. He has been a regular contributor to
Hanging Loose since 1980. His poems have appeared in
*Main Street Rag, Off The Coast, Bayou Magazine, Slant,
Tipton Poetry Journal, Cholla Needles* and many others.
He has published three volumes of poetry: *Three New
Poets (Hanging Loose Press), Denny's Arbor Vitae
(Adelaide Books)* and *Carrying Bodies (Main Street Rag
Press)*. He lives in Wisconsin with his husband of 21 years.

The Dream-Shadow

Emily Bilman

After we broke up, the cloak of forgetfulness
Wrapped me within its soft fur, lulling me to sleep.
Asleep by the river bank, your virtual face
Appeared among the reeds, an apparition

So much resembling you, I still believe
It was the real you standing next to me
While your shadow watched me sleep
And your dark presence disturbed my dream.

Upon waking, I remembered my wound:
Like a protean child afraid to commit yourself,

You procrastinated, preferring your bird-flight
To our twin-song until we fell apart.

Come, my love, let us restore
The frayed filaments of our lost love.
Come, my love, let's stitch our tattered attires
Into a fabric patterned by our desire.

Dr. Emily Bilman teaches poetry in Geneva as
London's Poetry Society's Stanza representative in
Switzerland. Her dissertation, *The Psychodynamics of
Poetry: Poetic Virtuality and Oedipal Sublimation in
the Poetry of T.S. Eliot and Paul Valéry* was published
by Lambert Academic in 2010 and *Modern Ekphrasis*
in 2013 by Peter Lang. Her poetry books, *A Woman By
A Well* (2015), *Resilience* (2015), and *The Threshold
of Broken Waters* (2018) were published by
Troubador, UK. Poems were published in *The London
Magazine, Poetry Salzburg Review, Offshoots, San Antonio Review, Expanded
Field, Poetics Research, Oxford School of Poetry Review, Subterranean Blue Poetry*.
She blogs on http://www.emiliebilman.wix.com/emily-bilman

Stone Calendar

Ziaeddin Torabi

We went to visit Mayans
 in a faraway city
 with lots of hotels
along the street
parallel to the seashore.

The seashore on which Mayans have walked
and the sea from which they fished.

 But, instance of Mayans, today
 people have come from four corners of the world,
they neither walk nor fish.

they lay down in the seaside, and sunbathing,
and when they became tired
they go to the sea, to swim.
hidden from the eyes of Mayans.

The Mayans who have gone into hidden in jungles
Getting alone with their ancient God
and the sun that always shining

over the splendid temple had made
with ninety nine steps at each four sides
as the symbol of four seasons of year,
and the last day,
has been located is on the top of the temple
as the symbol of the Sun -God.

The symbol that when the wandering tourists,
tired of sunbathing, go and visit .

The temple, that Mayans had made for their sacrificial ceremonies,
which is a stone calendar,
with a three hundred and sixty- five days,
intact.

And the rays of the sun
at the first day of the new year,
make a river of light,
from the top to the bottom of the temple,
crawling like a snake,
as the symbol of the Sun- God.

Ziaeddin Torabi is an Iranian-American poet living in
Sacramento who has published more than 30 books in different
areas, including poetry, translation, criticism, and review. From
1988-1998, he was the head of the Tehran Municipal Cultural
Center, and from 1999-2009, he taught Literature at the
University of Applied Sciences and Technology in Tehran. He
has won many literary awards, including the 2010 Iran Annual
Book Prize for his poetry collection, *Face To Face with Dreams*,
published in English translation by *Ad Lumen Press*.

Writer's Block

James Croal Jackson

You tell me you haven't
written for a long time.
I know. I know. I know.
Same. We continue on
our personal eternities
into forests to forget we
were a trickling sap
yet draw our bodies
against an oak in a
place where no one
knows. Dark corner of
the dark. I used to feed
on the bark of our getting
to know each other. Fine.
It's nighttime. A fire
fly ambles through
the air, lands on my hand
and you ask for a jar.

James Croal Jackson has a chapbook, *The Frayed Edge of Memory* (Writing Knights Press, 2017), and poems in *Pacifica, indefinite space,* and *Philosophical Idiot.* He edits *The Mantle.* Currently, he works in the film industry in Pittsburgh. jimjakk.com

Emptiness

Bruce Levine

Past the keyhole
The portal to the unknown
Flowers bloom and signify
Lessons learned

Yet future unplanned
Remains unspoken
Time alone withstands the test
Of reality

Foraging through the inexplicable
Toward a new reality
Without a helping hand to guide
Its destiny

Questions remain
As sociology and psychology
Scramble through empty strata
Of perplexity

Fighting new platitudes
Unknown explanations
Diversity notwithstanding
No clarity

Lost communication
Through evolution
Of a backlit screen
Revealing nothing

Remain Silent

Bruce Levine

I stay,
go,
stand,
sit,
walk,
remain still,
sleep,
wake,
laugh,
cry,
speak,
remain silent.

Bruce Levine, a 2019 Pushcart Prize Poetry Nominee, has spent his life as a writer of fiction and poetry and as a music and theatre professional. His literary catalogue includes four novels, short stories, humorous sketches, flash fiction, poetry, essays, articles and a screenplay. Nearly 150 of his works are published in over 25 on-line journals including *Ariel Chart, Friday Flash Fiction, Literally Stories*; over 30 print books including *Poetry Quarterly, Haiku Journal, Dual Coast Magazine*, and his  shows have been produced in New York and around the country. His 7 eBooks are available from Amazon.com. His work is dedicated to the loving memory of his late wife, Lydia Franklin. He lives in New York with his dog, Daisy. Visit him at www.brucelevine.com.

The Gold Ford

Barbara Daniels

I see rings of insects, midges,
are they? And last night's rain
thrown down from trees, radiant

at the start of a long day of sunlight.
I walk through a corridor of trees,
looking left, looking right.

Dad burned fallen leaves. He planted
strawberries, rhubarb, corn.
Drove a black car. Then another.

"Cars should be black," he told me.
But even he went on to own
a gold Ford jostled and scratched

by bighorn sheep in the Rockies.
Monarch butterflies, hundreds, flew
to its hot surface and rested

on paint bright as an egret's feet.
Dad kissed Mom's lips as he lay
on a gurney. Maybe her name

was gone. But joy roused him
like sunlight and he grinned.
Yellow weeds lift blooms

toward the sun, day shadowed
by spikes of pine, Dad's bones
cold in the quiet ground.

The Veteran

Barbara Daniels

He knows he won't find enemies
stationed in long rows of trees,
but he must walk there. The food

and water of battle have not been cut
from his hair and nails or lost
in sloughed-off cells. Bile rises.

He swallows it, hears a pulse
at an odd high frequency
and the beating of his heart.

He's in his homeland. It's only
a stand of pines. He picks
his way among fallen branches,

beer cans, sodden paper, his fingers
pressed to his cheekbones. He
touches tree buds set to unfurl

in the distant spring. All his life
he dreamed of crossing a bridge
that ends abruptly over dark water.

Many nights he clings to cold
girders, then wakes as he
plunges to bursting waves.

Barbara Daniels' book *Rose Fever* was published by *WordTech Press* and chapbooks *Black Sails, Quinn & Marie,* and *Moon Kitchen* by *Casa de Cinco Hermanas Press.* Her poetry has appeared in *Prairie Schooner, Mid-American Review,* and elsewhere. She received three fellowships from the New Jersey State Council on the Arts.

Photo Credit: Mark Hillringhouse.

The Kids' Tree

Alex DeBonis

When the kindergarten teacher had us draw trees,
    I didn't sketch gray limbs, snow sugaring their tops.

I didn't color in rust speckles or the flames of mid-October
    nor branches studded with buds in late winter.

No, like the boy next to me, I copied *the* tree, that one anybody
    can draw, the cartoon in every kid's mental warehouse:

on a grass plain, jutting into blue with tufts of wool,
    brown trunk seamed in black, green blotches for leaves,

roots clutching the horizon as if a cyclone might rip it away.
    I drew the other kids' tree like I wanted another

kid's name, something inhabitable that draws no notice,
    a beige motel room of a moniker, not my surname

with its bloat of *D* and *B*, a buffoon with a tuba honking
    in my signature. Not those loops flopping over

the dotted line. I left my name off, so that picture could be
    mistaken for any other in the forest posted on the wall.

I wish I'd had the nerve to depict my tree floating free,
    a hyphen between root ball and spread of boughs.

What might have grown on that paper I didn't sign?
    Firebolts arcing from a stalk as tall as a skyscraper,

a maple that waves from a bluejean pocket, a willow at an opera
    shedding quicksilver tears, an oak bent under the lurid light

of a flood, pinecones big enough to eclipse all Asia, or my name
    in tree form, bleats and hoots cast as wood curling?

And so today, decades on, I grant my name its bumble, its tangle,
    its otherworldly roots to snag the ankles of passersby.

That Toxicity

Alex DeBonis

Made of kiln-fired clay, in the toil
and fuss of moving into my first house,
it was an icon of a household god,
a confection glazed in yellow, Mom's frog,
wall-eyed with caution. After my mother
stormed off, it was hiding like a stowaway
behind boxes labeled *DISHES*—
smile wide enough with cheer that inside
you could wedge a scouring pad.
She hadn't mentioned the knickknack
nor uttered another word after I said
her president belonged in Hell. She left.
My house's wood jambs and doors seized,
their warm creaks and groans silenced,
poisoned by its gleaming skin.
But I wish I'd kept the frog.
What might have sprung from its lips?
A hymn to salve a wound,
a song casting auras of affection
over my linoleum and window frames
to revive them, a hopeful prophecy?
Some gifts can stop your heart.
After I crammed it in a trash bag,
that toxicity welled up beneath
packing tape and cardboard
—I knew that stillness couldn't last—
but right then I was marker and coffin,
and a grave opened wide within me.

Alex DeBonis teaches fiction writing and literature at Bethel University in West Tennessee, and his work has appeared in *Parade Magazine, Esquire, Tipton Poetry Journal,* and *Hartskill Review.*

Presby Slagger

Scott T. Hutchison

was something my grandpa referred to as an *oddfellow*. Presby
didn't bother anybody: silent fourth-grader folded into the back row,
looking at books about the Wild West, while we spit-balled
each other, him every once in a while. David Fetty claimed
he'd seen him tagging along after his kooky mama out in public,
Presby wearing a white cowboy hat. Kid couldn't have been too dumb
not to wear it in school near us blackhearts. Apparently, the *Oddfellows*
were also a fraternal lodge, a gathering of odd professions,
made all the more peculiar since, in spite of the mean old world,
they chose to follow noble values: love, charity, benevolence.
Grandpa claimed they upheld a sacred motto: *Visit the sick,*
relieve the distressed, bury the dead, educate the orphan. Symbols,
rituals, skeletal masks—all part of their ceremonial mystery. Presby
wasn't an orphan, and no one knew he was sick. Maybe the kid
looked a little flushed, peaked, but not even his parents suspected
the bullet lodged in thigh flesh for ninety-two days. Presby never
ran around with us at recess, kept on reading his Deadwood and cowboy books
without even covering up when we played "Slag the Slagger,"
firing acorns at him from twenty paces back. Him sitting, smiling,
reading nonchalantly in spite of our vicious assault, giving us no clue
to the red and black screams secretly streaking up and down his leg.
If an Oddfellow knew of such a child's distress, I imagine
he might have taken Presby's hand, told him not to worry about
his intrusions into the family's forbidden gun cabinet, push back
the dire warnings of belt-beatings for firearm curiosity, pinning on that
heirloom sheriff's star. Such a listener might have kept his face placid
when listening to Presby whisper his thoughts of taking his father's
antique six-shooter, tying it down, quick-drawing and hammer-fanning
six acorns out of the air, paid attention as Presby imagined such a powerful thing
and more--just before the .22 fumbled and discharged into his tiny muscle.
Presby proved strong enough to keep it hidden for three months; his father
later admitted to strapping the uncrying kid four maybe five times
during his final fevered weeks--for sluggishness. The Slaggers had guns
and a tin star and no money; the Oddfellows covered the funeral. There
I discovered my grandfather was a virtuous and hidden man. He whisked me
and the boys to the side of that hard-dug hole, said "Sadly, we're dying out.
Perhaps you young men, one day, will embrace the Mystery." I loved
my grandfather--my only noble grace. Odd that he thought he saw something
righteous in us. Neither me nor my gathering of desperados even knew the word
"benevolence" and we sure as hell weren't going to look it up.
We saw Presby's waxen face in a casket. We saw his hand
grabbing pearl-handles, aiming, we saw the dead in his eye.

Scott T. Hutchison is a New Hampshire poet. Previous work has appeared in *The
Georgia Review* and *The Southern Review*. Poems are forthcoming in *Appalachian
Heritage, Concho River Review, Louisiana Literature, The Naugatuck River
Review, Red Dirt Forum, Steam Ticket* and *Tar River Poetry*. A new book of poetry,
Moonshine Narratives, is available from Main Street Rag Publishing.

Laundry Line

Holly Brazzle

On Mondays,
long after denim is dawned
and men milled,
before the sun's critical eye,
she hoists laundry—like hand washed
battle flags—on the line.

With one hand on line,
holding shoulders and waists in place,
she removes pin after pin
from between
pressed lips and clenched teeth.

Pin pinched,
with index and thumb, she
fortifies her formation:

Shells—fabric bodies
at attention, closing ranks
for inspection:

squaring slack
and singeing Irish Pennants:

pulling wrinkles from time
and creating in her image.

Holly Brazzle is a poet and an all-encompassing art
enthusiast. She has been published in the *Penwood Review*
and is in the process of completing a collection of ekphrastic
poetry. Brazzle is completing an MA in English and Creative
Writing program through Southern New Hampshire
University. She does not claim to have a home but is
currently residing in Germany with her husband and four
children.

Bring Them On

Gene Twaronite

He ...has endeavored to bring on the inhabitants of our frontiers, the merciless Indian Savages whose known rule of warfare, is an undistinguished destruction of all ages, sexes and conditions.
        — Declaration of Independence, July 4, 1776.

We painted them red
like the coats
of our oppressors,
then turned them
into savages.

We fought them in
undistinguished
destruction of
all ages, sexes
and conditions,
starved them into
submission,
then herded them
onto barren lands far
from their ancestors.

We clipped their braids
and forbade their
native tongues,
browbeat them
to conform
and acculturate.

We could have
brought them on
and made real peace
with justice for all.
We could have
listened and learned
new ways of living
on the sacred earth.

We could have
brought forth a new
country of united
nations—Apache,
Arapahoe, Blackfeet,
Cherokee, Crow,
Hopi, Hualapai,
Iowa, Kiowa,
Mohegan, Navaho,
Narragansett,
Paiute, Pequot, Pueblo,
Seminole, Zuni—
over five hundred strong
who could have
been there to help
us new immigrants
assimilate.

There are currently 573 tribes federally recognized by the Bureau of Indian Affairs.

Finalist

Gene Twaronite

We are all finalists in
contests we've never entered
You could be a winner
for the most times a person
used the same line
with no success or shame
for the most countries visited
while still asleep
for the most injustices
witnessed without
recognizing a single one
for the most
(choose category)
stupid, cruel, or vapid
things uttered
in one lifetime
for the most times you
chose the wrong door
and traded your humanity
for some dubious prize

Gene Twaronite a Tucson poet and the author of seven books, including two short story collections and two juvenile fantasy novels. His first book of poetry *Trash Picker on Mars* was published by Kelsay Books, and was the winner of the 2017 New Mexico/Arizona Book Award for Arizona poetry. His newest collection is *The Museum of Unwearable Shoes.*

From the Beginning

Edward Lee

Coating the soles
of my feet,
is the soil
I will be buried in.

It comforts me,
knowing it is there,
its grains and lumps,
its damp warmth.

It comforts me, too,
knowing everyone has some
touching the soles
of their feet, present
since birth, though
they are too busy
to feel its touch, its permanence,
too busy moving
so they might live,
too busy living
so they never stop,

never stop
and feel
the soil on their soles,
and the gentle comfort it brings,
the surety of what comes
no matter the steps taken.

Edward Lee poetry, short stories, non-fiction and photography have been published in magazines in Ireland, England and America, including *The Stinging Fly, Skylight 47, Acumen* and *Smiths Knoll*. Edward lives in Ireland. His debut poetry collection *Playing Poohsticks On Ha'Penny Bridge* was published in 2010. He is currently working towards a second collection. He also makes musical noise under the names *Ayahuasca Collective, Lewis Milne, Orson Carroll, Blinded Architect, Lego Figures Fighting,* and *Pale Blond Boy*. His Facebook page can be found at www.facebook.com/edwardleewriter.

Withering

Marie Gray Wise

What to do with each day
is a problem
no one waiting
no schedule-harness

thoughts for improvement
now that there's time
melt, dissolve, wither
before action

this stab
into this genre
so dangerous
for what it slices open

dolorous repetitions
of a haunting year
fear fomenting in the gut
longing and hope outlawed

a bloom of regret
endlessly propagating
refusing to wither
into a natural state

Marie Gray Wise's work has appeared in *U.S. 1 Worksheets, The Café Review, Naugatuck River Review, Grey Sparrow Journal, The Paterson Literary Review,* and *English Journal.*

Tats

William Greenway

Only carnies had them—hard-bitten,
cigarette-lipped, cadaverous—
and sailors and soldiers, of course.
Back when I got drunk on shore leave
in San Diego, I'd have gotten one too,
if I hadn't passed out.
My lifer buddies could've fixed me good:
an anchor wearing my wife's name,
or a heart swearing Semper Fi,
dooming me to a future of bar fights
with Marines who loved to knock off
our Dixie Cups, or with bikers, death skulls
on their skinheads.

And then it was the Age of Aquarius: Now!
on the wrist, twining rose on the ankle,
The Great Mandala, Child
of the Universe, and other such stuff.

Now, what is left? Zen wisdom
from a fortune cookie—Chinese
calligraphy for kung pao chicken—
Celtic armbands of wannabe warriors,
symbols of tribes or teams,
the tramp stamps of the doggie position?

And what will be left? This End Up?,
Gone But Not Forgotten?,
the multicolored county fair
hot-air balloon of ascension,
cocoon of resurrection,
the butterflies on shrink-wrapped skin
now shriveled into Rorschach blots
open to any interpretation.

A Few Thoughts on Death

William Greenway

My daughter's new toy
is my blood-pressure cuff,
which she pumps until
she triumphantly announces,
"You're dead!"
Then I head- and tongue-loll,
though my eyes must remain closed
as if I am sleeping,
but the blue pallor is beyond
the skill of the living.

On the drive home from kindergarten
yesterday, a skunk
crossed the road in front of me,
no need to guess about
this old man's omen.

The other parents look like
they're about 16, fathers
trendy with buzz cuts and beards,
their wives chubby
with perennial pregnancy.
They think I'm the grandfather,
and I could have been if
I hadn't thought children
an anchor, instead of a lifeboat.
Nothing worse than an old timer
with new regrets.

So when she asked me what death is,
I blathered on about endless sleep,
of Grandma in heaven, or
someplace of equivalent beauty
(or boredom), and when she asked
if it is going to hurt, I say no,
and hope, for her at least, it's quick,

just another Little Old Ladybug
on God's Great Windshield,
and pray that her next death
be like the first, that slippery slide
down, from the kinder garden of Eden,
a long dark tunnel
toward a rumor of light.

William Greenway's *Selected Poems* is from FutureCycle
Press and his newest and twelfth collection is *The Accidental
Garden* from Word Press. His collections, *Everywhere at
Once* and *Ascending Order* (both from University of Akron
Press Poetry Series) won Poetry Book of the Year Awards from
the Ohio Library Association. His poems have appeared in
*American Poetry Review, Poetry, Missouri Review, Southern
Review, Georgia Review, Southern Poetry Review, Prairie
Schooner, Poetry Northwest,* and *Shenandoah.* He has won
numerous awards including Georgia Author of the Year. He is
Distinguished Professor of English Emeritus at Youngstown
State University and lives in Ephrata, Pennsylvania.

Arizona Sunset

John Grey

The west's gold-plated.
The east is up-front with its darkness.
In the north,
rust-red clouds move on,
leaving nothing to our advantage.
The sky burns away to the south.
The desert sleeps with dark and light,
embedded down with mountains.
A few wildflowers on the trail,
some purple, some pink,
speak for other hues.
A lizard, a mouse,
welcome the cooling,
prod and poke in dry grasses,
gleaned by power eyes of eagles.
It's a harsh land
daubed in color and life.
Hard earth, creosote and rock pile...
no canvas is wasted.

First Solo

John Grey

The boat is old
but the water's still
and not so deep.
From pirates to storms at sea,
a boy can imagine
what else is needed.

The rowing is hard
on unformed muscle.
The oars don't so much skim
as slug it out with the surface.

The mallards are unperturbed.
The boy seems more of a threat
to himself than to waterfowl.
They drift away more out of habit than fear.

His father watches from the bank.
Last time out, the two of them
sailed the seven seas together.
But this is a solo crossing.

Sadly, he rows to close
to the reeds, the cattails.
Blackbirds gurgle their familiar conk-a-ree
at the boys dilemma.
He's stuck.
More effort merely turns him
in a half-circle.

His father is soon wading the water.
Rescue is on the way.

Growing up will have to wait.

John Grey is an Australian poet, US resident in Rhode Island. Recently published in *Midwest Quarterly, Poetry East* and *North Dakota Quarterly* with work upcoming in *South Florida Poetry Journal, Hawaii Review* and the *Dunes Review*.

At Dusk

Alex MacConochie

The sound's a violet, rippled parachute.
Doing backstroke, you're translucent

Where the sun pours through your fingers
Bright as laughter: it's not cold!

We don't know, but will find out soon
I followed you in with my phone in a pocket

And spent how long warming up, the inns,
Homes island-side fading into lights.

Falmouth Main Street

Alex MacConochie

Long loose tunics, plaids and paisleys, blow
On a sale rack in the awning shadow: dapple
A shopper's hands with hues that, blending, fade.

A millstone, with a concrete-stoppered hole
Where its many petals join, now's a sunlit bench
At Town Hall: a ground from grinding, useful thing.

People are apologizing, stepping right
Then right to go around each other, laughing
As they move too soon and, nervous, then too slow—

A native of Norfolk, Virginia, **Alex MacConochie** currently lives and writes in
Somerville, Massachusetts. His poems appear in *Tar River Poetry, The Summerset
Review, Louisiana Literature, Constellations,* and elsewhere.

Good Luck in a Bad Place

Paul Lojeski

He'd wake in the middle of the night to see Larry
doing chin-ups off the cell bars.

During the day they sat at a metal table, smoking
and playing cards.

Or he'd watch him pace back and forth, punching
air like a boxer warming up before a fight.

Later, on a beach, a child touches his face and a choir
of gulls sing fabled songs.

Friendship

Paul Lojeski

Frank called to say George
was going soon. That he'd
refused more treatments:
they were useless, nothing
would cure him now or even
make him more comfortable.
So he'd taken to bed at home,
seeking dignity and moments
of serenity. Visitors streamed
in, taking turns holding his
hand, small talking it towards
the end. Frank told me this
on the way over to say goodbye, to take George's warm
hand in his: skin-to-skin,
blood-to-blood, death-to-death.

Paul Lojeski was born and raised in Lakewood, Ohio. He attended Oberlin College. His poetry has appeared online and in print. He lives in Port Jefferson, New York.

Bella Señorita

Erren Geraud Kelly

if playing the piano were like breathing
she would be the oxygen flowing
happily through my veins
i mistake her for a french woman
but she is spanish
but she could easily look
french
every word that comes from
her mouth is a poem
her hair is black as a
raven's wing
and she walks like she plays
chopin
her fingers strolling across the
keyboard
as i imagine we could be doing
along the streets of seville
 or madrid
if i were picasso, i would
paint her the way she plays
in long, broad strokes,
always abstract
which would be an accomplishment
since i'm a concrete poet
though like dali, sometimes,
i allow my mind to travel
outside of my body
i want to feel her playing the
" clar de lune,"
even as the night gives us wings.

Erren Geraud Kelly's work has appeared in numerous
publications in print and online in various literary journals and
magazines throughout the United States, Canada and Europe.
Mr. Kelly is the author of the book Disturbing The Peace, on
Night Ballet Press. Erren received his BA in English – Creative
Writing from Louisiana State University in Baton Rouge. Kelly
lives in Los Angeles.

Kakegawa

William Doreski

We've crossed so many arched bridges
braced by spindly pilings. They all
seem too dramatic to span
those lazy tidal rivers
no sailboats try to navigate.

Windy today. Everyone walking
West leans into the draft. Those
with the weather at their backs
slog along unconcerned, one fellow
even holding a fan, ready
to concoct his own private breeze
should the natural one desist.

There's Mount Akiba sporting
its famous shrine. But you're eyeing
the kite some wag has lofted,
a disc of paper with a long tail.
And look, there's another, chasing
itself, loose and lost in the sky.

Kusatsu

William Doreski

A green, house-shaped palanquin.
Another one, open to reveal
its occupant crouched like a toad.

In the background, the rice-cake shop
serves a dozen customers,
their faces anonymous with hunger,

traveling clothes rumpled and dusty.
Here the road to the mountains forks off,
confusing those lacking maps.

The porters toting their loads
are almost naked, allowing their sweat
to grease the roadway and smooth

the way for those who follow.
Not all the rice cakes in Japan
could make their labor worthwhile.

William Doreski teaches writing and literature at Keene State
College in New Hampshire. His work has appeared in various
journals and in sevelera collections, most recently *The Suburbs of
Atlantis* (AAA Press, 2013).

Passed Down
Sem Megson

Her kitchen shelves, repurposed wood on iron brackets, sit
in the sun's path through an open window. There,
among her dishes, rough plastic cups scatter light.
They were passed down to her with scars
of teeth on the rims. Hunger eats into surfaces malleable as skin.
For her at eighty, these heirlooms—my word, not hers—
equal silver goblets with Lion Passants. What's more,
their scars have transmuted over the years
to become an indication of worth. She knows
her people bit into water to feed the work of their hands.
They bore the brunt, sweeping the earth
for another's jewels. Nothing fell sparkling into their cups
like sunlight. She is warmed by their memories
glowing through this bond of generations. It is a part
of her own coming to terms. Her hands hold
where their fingers held, a grandfather, a cousin, a matriarch
wrapping tight. Her lips press into their mould,
coiled as DNA. She is in the history of their hallmarks.

Sem Megson's poetry and plays have been published and produced in the United States, the United Kingdom, and Canada. Sem lives in Toronto. For more information, visit <u>semmegson.com</u>.

Palimpsest
Frank Modica

Suppose you
tattooed your life
on broad stretches
of arm, back,
stomach, thigh—
intricate pictures,
of your deeds

good and bad,
hoping to pass
on the stories
to your children.

After your death
will the family
keep those tales
and gather every year,
dragging out your carcass
to retell them—

or will they scrape off
those old tattoos
and stencil their
own epics?

Frank Modica is a retired public school teacher in Urbana, Illinois. He taught students with special needs for 34 years. Since his retirement he volunteers with a number of arts and social service organizations in his community. His work has appeared in *Spindrift Literary Arts Journal, Slab, Heyday Magazine, Cacti Fur Magazine, The Tishman Review, Crab Fat Literary Magazine,* and *Black Heart Magazine.*

Saints & Sinners

Robin Ray

Who can deny the heart is a serious warrior
when oleanders and scarlet pimpernels bloom
in my neighbor's lawn, warships and missile

silos rumble in mine? I flood my bald spot
with Rogaine hoping to fool mother's nature
into gifting me bedroom hair. In my worse

derailment, that is, before I've recovered from
the slip of time, the crack of tumbling dikes,
I funnel through esplanades of extremes. Hot

is a firing pin, cold is physics, warmth an
illusion. Saints are rich in charity, sinners in
vanity, no diversity but them. Between brown

and grizzly, I choose panda. Kiang and onager,
zebra. Magpie and pelican, penguin. Colors of
the rainbow, grayer than I remember. Autumn,

soft as nerds, still a hard precursor to the holidays.
Unlike you who see light at the end, or a shimmer,
or shine, I behold the deepest black of all, awakening.

Robin Ray, formerly of *Trinidad & Tobago*, resides in Port Townsend, Washington.
His works have appeared at *Red Fez, Scarlet Leaf Review, Aphelion, Spark,
Neologism Poetry Journal*, and elsewhere.

First Panic Attack This Month

Chris Pellizzari

Hunting dogs trample through my mental illness
childhood memories escape like pheasants from the brush
shot down by hunters
who do not eat what they kill.

Exploding feathers of defense mechanisms
fall from gunpowder sky.

A shot heard around the world
does not even create an echo in
the vortex of burning trees
falling into themselves.

Hunters carrying dead birds by the claws
as if they were pulled up from the earth like carrots.

Plucked and wings removed
it is hard to imagine they could fly
in previous lives.

Dropped in the pot as meat
to feed me my illness.

Chris Pellizzari is a graduate of the University of
Illinois at Urbana-Champaign. His work has appeared in
numerous literary magazines, including
*COUNTERCLOCK, Schuylkill Valley Journal, Open:
Journal of Arts & Letters,* and *Allegro Poetry Magazine.*
He is a member of *The Society of Midland Authors* and is
assistant editor at *The Awakenings Review.* Chris lives
in Illinois.

Writing Among Life
John Timothy Robinson

All these lines in wrath-rapt syllables,
verbal carving unlike chiseled stone.
The words should sing though not disable,
dark affliction taken in bone
rendering cadence impossibly made.
At times, people want to be alone,
without laughter in sun-dappled shade.
So, you take a drive, a walk, put down the phone.
Everything seems fine, just then, while
the dog barks, dinner is cold, late,
your children made murals on kitchen tile.
You made pieces of your favorite plate.
Somehow, regardless, things fall together
in an order of another order, a pillow's feather.

John Timothy Robinson is a mainstream poet of the expressive image and
inwardness from the Kanawha Valley in Mason County, West Virginia. His poetics
was developed in the tradition of James Wright, Rita Dove, Donald Hall, Marvin
Bell, Maxine Kumin, WS Merwin, Tess Gallagher and Robert Bly among many
others. John's works have appeared in ninety-nine journals throughout the United
States, Canada, the United Kingdom and India. He is also a published printmaker
with eighty-two art images and photographs appearing in journals, electronic and
print in the United States, Italy and Ireland.

Around Moose Jaw
Richard Luftig

The two old guys sit down
at their regular table near
the chalkboard that announces:
Two eggs, toast, potatoes, bacon, drink—
$7.95 as the waitress, probably pushing
eighty herself, comes over, pours
them coffee and says You're late.

God, this is the place where I want
to stay forever. But one can only drink
so many refills of coffee before
exploding, so I take my leave,
walk past the four-post Hamilton
Beach milkshake blender with two
posts permanently dead. Can't get parts
for them anymore the owner says as he rings

me up, takes two pennies from the paper cup
next to the register to round off my bill,
gives me a Canadian one-dollar Looney
and two-dollar Tooney for my change.
I walk outside to the sign announcing tours
through the tunnels under Main Street where
Al Capone is said to have hid

his bootlegged whiskey, then register
at the Capone Hotel with the machine gun
shaped sign. I ask the manager if people really visit
this Saskatchewan town just to see where Capone
was supposed to have hung out and if it's all made up.

A damn lot more than if we didn't say he did, he says.

Later, I drive a quarter-mile out of town
where everything are flat fields broken
only by the sweet shadows
of windbreak trees hundreds of yards apart.
Afternoon fills the air with striads
of heat, where the wheat breathes
into a gentle, west-Canadian wind
their own summer poems.

Richard Luftig is a former professor of educational psychology and special education at Miami University in Ohio now residing in California. His poems and stories have appeared in numerous literary journals in the United States (INCLUDING *TIPTON POETRY JOURNAL* and internationally in Canada, Australia, Europe, and Asia. Two of his poems recently appeared in *Realms of the Mothers: The First Decade of Dos Madres Press*. His latest book of poems is available from *Unsolicited Press in 2019*. His webpage and blog may be found at richardluftig.com

Vessels

Gil Hoy

When you're
a bottle,

twenty-nine
years

can go
by fast--

not necessarily so
for a little girl.

Through Hurricane
    Hugo

 The whipping winds
   The crashing rain

The stones that missed

You, you survived
intact

To tell the tale

Of an eight-year
old girl

Who skipped
along the beach

On that
happy weekend,

Twenty-nine
years ago,

To put
a note
deep inside
of you

Before hurling you
deep inside
the sea.

For she
was the maker
of her note,

The paper now
slightly stained,

The ink now
somewhat smudged.

And you were
the holder
of the song
she sang,

You, now
covered with
the trappings
of the sea:

Shelled sea creatures

Affixed tightly
to your surface

Green and red
plants

That only
grow in
the sea.

She, having
long since
moved out
of her

Childhood home,
and having
long since

forgotten
about you.

Our little girl
lay awake
at night

For weeks
in her bed,

After that
happy weekend,

Thinking about you
and waiting

For a response
that never came.

Or should
I say
came late,

When she was
no longer

A little girl,
and the world

Had become
a very

different place.

Gil Hoy is a Boston poet and semi-retired trial lawyer studying poetry at Boston University through its Evergreen program. Hoy previously received a B.A. in Philosophy and Political Science from Boston University, an M.A. in Government from Georgetown University, and a J.D. from the University of Virginia School of Law. He served as a Brookline, Massachusetts Selectman for four terms. Hoy's poetry has appeared in *Chiron Review, The New Verse News, Ariel Chart, Social Justice Poetry, The Potomac, The Penmen Review* and elsewhere.

Loving the Dead
Helga Kidder

The cardinal said, *she lives*
between the sun and the moon,
within the light of stars.

Each rose petal says,
she is here, opening the flower
to perfection. Her voice
whispering the wind,
unfolding your heart.

The mirror reflects her shadow
behind you. *Don't grieve.*
You are not alone.

Not in the woods or fields.
Not in the city.
She is turning down her bed
inside you.

Helga Kidder lives in the Tennessee hills with her husband and dog. She was awarded an MFA from Vermont College and am co-founder of the Chattanooga Writers Guild. Her poems have been published in *Haight Ashbury Literary Journal, Poetry South, Slipstream*, and in *Carrying the Branch: Poets in Search of Peace* anthology. Helga has three poetry books: *Wild Plums, Luckier than the Stars*, and *Blackberry Winter*.

One, Two, Three
Keith Welch

The first was my father, a man who
skipped high school, joined the navy,
sailed the world, saw no action.

No fighting, anyway— whether
he saw any other sort of action,
I never knew.

Absent often, a factory man rotating
his shifts at DuPont downtown, he retired early
to bag groceries at Wegmans. An unhandy man
both with tools and marriage, within his bland
exterior he nursed a volatile temper.

He was a god until I saw him cry—
then he was only a man.

I myself have never married.

The second husband was a big man, orchard man,
expansive as one of his apple trees. His hands
were easily twice the size of mine, and I rejected him
out-of-hand as a father figure. A slow talker,
he had a long line of fatherly advice, which I resented.
Handy as all get-out, as farmers often are, he died
slowly, by degrees, as big men often do.

I've never had the urge to marry.

The third husband and I never met.
Emerging from among the parishioners
of my mother's church—
met, married, and deceased
before we faced each other.

One, two, three: what did they have
missing in my unbroken heart?

The Tree

Keith Welch

I confess— I killed the locust tree
that loomed above the house. Testing me
by splitting from crotch to root,
it had to come down, so was felled,

dismembered, and spirited away
on trailers. One day strong
and leaf-full, the next a sprinkling
of sawdust around a pathetic stump.

The tree has become a cliche:
the thing unappreciated until gone.
The newly naked yard cowers under
the glare of an unhindered summer sun.

Could I have coerced the great
crack together with straps,
with winches, with steel cable?
With kind words, with hexes, with songs?

It might have survived split open for years,
crooked like two elders leaning on canes.
Or, like a clumsy giant, torn a corner
off my home. I miss the tree like I miss

the dogs that died in the road outside
my childhood home. Like the lost books
that have sheltered me from a caustic world.

Closing Time

Keith Welch

My small town can't restrain itself--
randy and insatiable, it muffin-tops
into the countryside, shedding landmarks
as it bulges outward.

The corporate bookstore where I used to loiter
drinking coffee has closed. I read
their magazines, hardly ever bought
their books, so: my bad.

Our Waffle House went years ago
swept aside for condominia erupting
from the ground like wood volcanoes,
erasing the sun, creating canyons.

You can't live in the memory of a town.
One day I will step off a bus and be lost
on an expired map of a nonexistent city.

And when I die, who will remember
that little red hotdog stand
in the parking lot
next to the bank?

The Mother Visit

Keith Welch

She remembers me
as a night of passion
as an abdominal anomaly
as a sputtering infant
as a sullen teen
as an absent adult.

Inner voice, keeper
of my prehistory, She sets
my worn feet back into
their primal footprints.

Origin of the world,
redeemer of my failures
as a son, forgiver of my
fault of independence,

she rolls up her life
at the ends, taking
history with her, needing
no pity,

And When she's gone, will
I be like a kite
without a string?

Keith Welch lives in Bloomington, Indiana where he works at the Indiana University Herman B Wells library. He has poems published in *The Tipton Poetry Journal, Open: Journal of Arts & Letters, Dime Show Review, and Literary Orphans*, among others. He enjoys complicated board games, baking, talking to his cat, Alice, and meeting other poets. His website is keithwelchpoetry.com

Disappearing Pages

Jack Lorts

I'm noticing the pages
disappearing,
silently slipping away,
words dissolving
into dust.

The horizon evaporating
into the sky,
and I not noticing.

Days departing
into silence,
into not remembering.

I'm seeing pages
floating about in the wind,
not knowing where
they are going,
where they've been.

It's especially hard
for poets,
seeing words disappear,
slip away,
dissolve,
evaporate.

I'm noticing the pages
disappearing.

A retired educator living in a small town in Eastern Oregon, **Jack E. Lorts** has appeared extensively, if infrequently, over the past 40+ years in such magazines as *Arizona Quarterly, Kansas Quarterly, English Journal, Agnostic Lobster* and *Fishtrap,* among others. Author of three chapbooks, T*he Daughter Poems & Others...* and *The Meeting-Place of Words*, published by Pudding House, and *Dear Gilbert Sorrentino & Other Poems* from Finishing Line Press.   Uttered Chaos Press of Eugene, Oregon recently published his *The Love Songs of Ephram Pratt*. Active in local and state Democratic politics, he served as Mayor of Fossil, Oregon for many years; currently lives in The Dalles, Oregon.

Light Rider

Iain Twiddy

It's not like memory is a runaway horse
hijacking, thundering, a juggernaut
racing against the horizon,

dumping me, broken-shouldered,
just a minute back in the past,
but trudging a lifetime to catch up.

More like the light rider, clinging on
above the horrendous
double-thud of the heart

implanting the fact of how long time has run,
how implacably I have galloped
like a runaway horse spooked by the sense

it is actually a man carrying, wherever he goes,
a weight of absence
heavier than everything yet to happen.

April Slush

Iain Twiddy

April slush blanching in the sun,
as if in none of the preceding months
it had ever dragged anybody down,
ever pulled or shoved the old over,
let alone cracked or smashed, separated bones,

while the leak from each heap, black on the concrete,
points the finger at where the ice encased,
a slur insisting they clearly weren't the same,
a censoring that only gets embellished
by the indifference of the rain.

Iain Twiddy studied literature at university and lived for several years in northern Japan. He has poems published or forthcoming in *Salamander, Quiddity, The Blue Mountain Review, The Dalhousie Review, Flyway* and elsewhere.

My Name is Neighbor

Duane Anderson

When I would see my neighbor,
one in particular,
which wasn't often,
he would just say 'Hi Neighbor'
like it was my name.
He never called me by my first name
though I was pretty sure I had one.
Maybe he couldn't remember my name,
or maybe he just didn't care to know it,
and I never bothered to ask.

To him I had a name,
it was Neighbor,
though at least he remembered
I was one of his neighbors,
but still, it made me wonder if he called all
his neighbors by the same name.
It sure would simplify his life

Emergency Rooms

Duane Anderson

In the past few weeks
I have visited four hospital emergency rooms
and many doctor's lobbies
waiting and waiting
while my wife gets poked and tested

trying to find out why she is feeling the pain
that she is going through,
and EKG's, stress tests, ultrasounds, x-rays, MRIs
are parts of the new norm.
The doctors rule out certain common problems

but so far, no diagnosis
on what is causing her issues
and my wife's stress grows
until an answer has been determined,
and then what comes next?

Will it go away on its own,
is there a procedure to correct it,
will there some medicine to take
for the rest of her life?
Many doctor visits, many questions remain

in her search for an answer.
In the meantime,
I wait in another hallway with
notebook and novel
trying to pass the time as best I can.

Duane Anderson currently lives in La Vista, Nebraska, and volunteers with the American Red Cross as a Donor Ambassador on their blood drives. He has had poems published in *Poetry Quarterly, Fine Lines, The Sea Letter, Cholla Needles, Wilderness House Literary Review, Adelaide Literary Magazine* and several other publications.

Mercy

Marianne Lyon

He was young once—
brown eyed, dewy cheeks
Now aged, he sits at my table
sometimes sunshine
knells through window
other days
rain stings against glass
I am repulsed
by thorny complaints
gruff laugh
swollen bitterness
I do not respond
push him from my concern
But today discarding
sour words squeezing into
sighs and fears
a door inside of me
falls open

A different response
traverses my heart.
Complaints and sneers
take on different timbre
Am I seeing
with mercy eyes?
Am I feeling
with compassion ears?

I look through his watery amber eyes
begin to see clues holding raw pain
My timid smile greets him
my head tilts
I ask him to stay on
heat kettle water

offer a cup of tea
look into still-wide-glaring
behold a frightened child
I must invite to play hop-scotch
coax to sing "Three Blind Mice"
Curious to know what some fun
might have done
had we shared it back then

Marianne Lyon has been a music teacher for 43 years. After teaching in Hong Kong, she returned to the Napa Valley and has been published in various literary magazines and reviews including *Ravens Perch, TWJM Magazine, Earth Daughters* and *Indiana Voice Journal.* She was nominated for the *Pushcart Prize* in 2017. She is a member of the *California Writers Club* and an Adjunct Professor at Touro University in California.

The Landscape Falters, Lost Meanings Re-Emerge

J.J. Steinfeld

I have a secret to share with you
(maybe not a secret, more like a contradiction
or a blundering confession)
something I learned in the artificial light
of anxiety and reshaping lost selves.

Well, you see, hope is infinite
hopelessness is thin as a knife blade
against your throat on a sun-filled day
the only thing that makes absolute sense
is senselessness and its cunning attendants.

The landscape falters, lost meanings re-emerge,
I'm still offering words and re-made dreams
with a flaw of archaeology occurring
in the terrain between truth and deception.

And the question remains
who will fall in first,
the one who reveals
or the one who hears
or both unceremoniously together?

Canadian poet, fiction writer, and playwright **J. J. Steinfeld** lives on Prince Edward Island, where he is patiently waiting for Godot's arrival and a phone call from Kafka. While waiting, he has published 19 books, including *Absurdity, Woe Is Me, Glory Be* (Guernica Editions, 2017), and *A Visit to the Kafka Café* (Ekstasis Editions, 2018). His short stories and poems have appeared in numerous periodicals and anthologies internationally, and over 50 of his one-act plays and a handful of full-length plays have been performed in Canada and the United States.

As I Understand You

Andrew Hamilton

             God
        I pray you will
forge my elemental
        self your selfless
key which unlocks
        solar grace
                cool wisdom
        humble strength
serving fellows
        from the mortal vessel
of your immortal wish
        for human kindness
afloat the spatial
        sea of your creation

             God
        I pray you will
free the carbon
        mind and body
from the selfish
        cage of desire

             God
        I pray you will
let me breathe
        God consciously
the terse minimalism
        of your seminal name

             God
        I pray you will
sanctify distress
        unlace each sugar chain
of carnal corruption
        anchored to my vessel

God
I pray you will
quench consumption
relinquish suffering
for everlasting sails
lifting gravity's need
to tranquil destinations
of your indigenous kind

God
I pray you will
open the earth—
—locked universe
wide with willing
doors which welcome
lunar love
bright restraint
modest mercy
breathing alive
your wholesome presence
of eternal days
and ageless nights

God
I pray you will
greet my being
with the nameless
introduction of living
deathless and free
oh my God
I pray you will

Amen

Andrew Hamilton graduated from Saint Mary's College of California with
his MFA. His work has appeared in The *Saturday Evening Post's* Great
American Fiction Contest, *Abstract Magazine TV*, *The Main Street Rag*, *Dream
Pop*, *Cleaver*,*Maudlin House*, *Blue Fifth Review*, and *Yes Poetry*
with new poems forthcoming in *Tule Review, I-70 Review, and Canyon
Voices*. He lives near Seattle where he counsels college transfer students
at Mercer Education while providing service work for the recovery community.

The arc

Patrick T. Reardon

It was efficient to
break the legs of the thieves
so their unsupported torsos
would slide down the wood
and cause their throats to
clutch for unobtainable air
until, in the course of things,
they were strangled
by the weight of their bodies,
a forced suicide.

The other was already dead.
His body was carried away.

Theirs, thrown into a ravine
to be pecked at by ugly talons and
gnawed at by dust insects and then
excreted in the nature of Nature.

I steal into this world and,
against my will,
get escorted out for
crashing the party.

I watch the scar-face
lift his sledgehammer
and measure the arc to my knees.

Patrick T. Reardon is the author of eight books, including the poetry collection *Requiem for David* and *Faith Stripped to Its Essence*, a literary-religious analysis of Shusaku Endo's novel *Silence*. Reardon, who worked as a Chicago Tribune reporter for 32 years, has published essays and book reviews widely in such publications as the Tribune, Chicago Sun-Times, Crain's Chicago Business, National Catholic Reporter and U.S. Catholic. His poems, nominated twice for a Pushcart Prize, have appeared throughout the U.S. as well as in Paris and India. His novella *Babe* was short-listed by Stewart O'Nan for the annual Faulkner-Wisdom Contest.

More Insect Logic

Michael Shepley

we live on now
the same as if
flying through Maytide
like stain glass
happy wing butterflies
in feeding frenzies
over fields of gold
where just yesterday
the buzzing dragonfly
by-plane plied the same
old poison stainrain
that Monsato sold

To put in more plain
in stronger cold English–
there's little chance
we shall dance on
too much longer

Botticelli Impression

Michael Shepley

in this earth
time iced impression
from some big
spotlight moon mirror
silver dollar midnight
she sat and sighed-
half shadowed not
quite peach skinned
creamy in the
cold wide light-
Venus on a half shell
sheet on saw edge
crude grass in a
crackerbox house backyard
seeming dissolute content
and enigmatic smiled
shifting her poetic ass
warm with regeneration
as the warm breeze
fingers combed her
wild Botticelli hair
calm again

Michael Shepley is a writer/researcher in Sacramento, California. His poems appeared in print in *California Quarterly, Muse International (India), Seems, Xanadu* and *DM du Jour*.

Editor

Barry Harris is editor of the *Tipton Poetry Journal* and two anthologies by Brick Street Poetry: *Mapping the Muse: A Bicentennial Look at Indiana Poetry* and *Words and Other Wild Things*. He has published one poetry collection, *Something At The Center*. Barry lives in Brownsburg, Indiana and is retired from Eli Lilly and Company. His poetry has appeared in *Kentucky Review, Valparaiso Poetry Review, Grey Sparrow, Silk Road Review, Saint Ann's Review, Boston Literary Magazine, Night Train, Silver Birch Press, Flying Island, Awaken Consciousness, Writers' Bloc,* and *Red-Headed Stepchild*. One of his poems was on display at the National Museum of Sport and another is painted on a barn in Boone County, Indiana as part of Brick Street Poetry's Word Hunger public art project. His poems are also included in these anthologies: *From the Edge of the Prairie; Motif 3: All the Livelong Day;* and *Twin Muses: Art and Poetry*.

Assistant Editor

Riley Childers is the assistant editor of the *Tipton Poetry Journal* for the Summer 2019 issue. She is in her final year at the University of Indianapolis studying Professional Writing, Creative Writing, and Digital Photography, and hopes to one day be a book editor and designer. Riley spends most of her time reading as many books as she possibly can, writing, and taking photos of her different adventures. She has found love for poetry through *Tipton Poetry Journal* and has been so thankful to be on the publication for this issue.

Contributor Biographies

Joe Albanese is a writer from South Jersey. His fiction, nonfiction, and poetry can be found in publications across the U.S. and in ten other countries. Joe is the author of *Smash and Grab, Caina, For the Blood is the Life, Candy Apple Red,* and a poetry collection, *Cocktails with a Dead Man.*

Duane Anderson currently lives in La Vista, Nebraska, and volunteers with the American Red Cross as a Donor Ambassador on their blood drives. He has had poems published in *Poetry Quarterly, Fine Lines, The Sea Letter, Cholla Needles, Wilderness House Literary Review, Adelaide Literary Magazine* and several other publications.

Dick Bentley's books, *Post-Freudian Dreaming, A General Theory of Desire, and All Rise* are available on Amazon. He won the Paris Writers/Paris Review's International Fiction Award and has published over 280 works of fiction, poetry, and memoir in the US, the UK, France, Canada, and Brazil. He served on the Board of the Modern Poetry Association and has taught at the University of Massachusetts. Find him online at www.dickbentley.com.

Dr. Emily Bilman teaches poetry in Geneva as London's Poetry Society's Stanza representative in Switzerland. Her dissertation, *The Psychodynamics of Poetry: Poetic Virtuality and Oedipal Sublimation in the Poetry of T.S. Eliot and Paul Valéry* was published by Lambert Academic in 2010 and *Modern Ekphrasis* in 2013 by Peter Lang. Her poetry books, *A Woman By A Well* (2015), *Resilience* (2015), *and The Threshold of Broken Waters* (2018) were published by Troubador, UK. Poems were published in *The London Magazine, Poetry Salzburg Review, Offshoots, San Antonio Review, Expanded Field, Poetics Research, Oxford School of Poetry Review, Subterranean Blue Poetry.* She blogs on http://www.emiliebilman.wix.com/emily-bilman

CL Bledsoe's most recent poetry collection is *Trashcans in Love.* He lives in northern Virginia with his daughter, and blogs, with Michael Gushue, at https://medium.com/@howtocvcn

Holly Brazzle is a poet and an all-encompassing art enthusiast. She has been published in the *Penwood Review* and is in the process of completing a collection of ekphrastic poetry. Brazzle is completing an MA in English and Creative Writing program through Southern New Hampshire University. She does not claim to have a home but is currently residing in Germany with her husband and four children.

Joseph Buehler has published 98 poems in *Nine Mile Magazine, Sentinel Literary Quarterly (U.K.), Ottawa Arts Review, Indiana Voice Journal, Otoliths (Australia), The Tower Journal, The Opiate, H.C.E. Review (Dublin), Angry Old Man Magazine, Common Ground Review, Blue Bonnet Review,* and others.. He is retired and lives in Georgia with his wife Trish. He was a finalist for the *Adelaide Literary Award in poetry (NYC)* in February and October 2018.

Roger Camp lives in Seal Beach, CA where he gardens, walks the pier, plays blues piano and spends afternoons with his pal, Harry, over drinks at Nick's on 2nd. When he's not at home, he's traveling in the Old World. His work has appeared in Pank, Southern Poetry Review and Nimrod.

Stephen Campiglio's poems and translations have recently appeared or are forthcoming in *Aji Magazine, Chiron Review, City Works Journal, Journal of*

Italian Translation, Manzano Mountain Review, Miramar, TAB: The Journal of Poetry & Poetics, and *Tipton Poetry Journal.* His new translation project is focused on the work of Italian poet, Giovanni Pascoli (1855-1912). A quarterfinalist in the 2018 Codhill Press poetry contest for a book-length manuscript and nominated for two Pushcart Prizes, Campiglio has published two chapbooks, *Cross-Fluence (2012)* and *Verbal Clouds through Various Magritte Skies (2014).*

Yvonne (aka Yvonne Chism-Peace) is the first poetry editor of two pioneer feminist magazines, *Aphra* and *Ms.* She has received several awards including two NEAs for poetry and a Leeway for fiction. Anthologies and annuals featuring her poems include: *Bryant Literary Review, Pinyon, Nassau Review 2019, Bosque Press #8, Foreign Literary Journal #1, Quiet Diamonds 2018, 161 One-Minute Monologues from Literature, This Sporting Life, Bless Me, Father: Stories of Catholic Childhood, Catholic Girls, Tangled Vines, Celebrations: A New Anthology of Black American Poetry, Pushcart Prize Anthology,* and *We Become New.* Yvonne lives in Philadelphia.

Gayle Compton writes about the most interesting and most misunderstood people in America, the common people of Eastern Kentucky--his people, from the hard-working to the bare-assed and proud. With a background in teaching and broadcasting he has been published in numerous journals and anthologies, including *Main Street Rag, Blue Mountain Review, U.S. 1 Worksheets,* and *Tipton Poetry Journal.* Gayle lives with his wife Sharon at Jonancy, Kentucky, the "Peabrook" setting for much of his work.

Katherine Cottle is a past contributor of the *Tipton Poetry Journal* and author of four full-length books--*The Hidden Heart of Charm City (forthcoming October 2019), I Remain Yours (2014), Halfway (2010),* and *My Father's Speech (2008),* all published by Apprentice House/Loyola University Maryland. More information can be found at www.katherinecottle.com

Barbara Daniels' book *Rose Fever* was published by *WordTech Press* and chapbooks *Black Sails, Quinn & Marie,* and *Moon Kitchen* by *Casa de Cinco Hermanas Press.* Her poetry has appeared in P*rairie Schooner, Mid-American Review,* and elsewhere. She received three fellowships from the New Jersey State Council on the Art.

Alex DeBonis teaches fiction writing and literature at Bethel University in West Tennessee, and his work has appeared in *Parade Magazine, Esquire, Tipton Poetry Journal, and Hartskill Review.*

William Doreski teaches writing and literature at Keene State College in New Hampshire. His work has appeared in various journals and in sevelera collections, most recently *The Suburbs of Atlantis* (AAA Press, 2013).

Donald Gasperson earned a Bachelor of Science degree in Psychology and a Master of Arts degree in Clinical Psychology working as a psychiatric rehabilitation counselor. After a lifetime of reading taking another step to writing was natural and self-affirming. Recognizing art in the insight at our fingertips was absorbing. He has had poetry published in *Quail Bell Magazine, The Bitchn" Kitsch, Big Windows Review, Foliate Oak Literary Review, Better Than Starbucks* and *Tipton Poetry Journal* among others. He lives in Klamath Falls, Oregon.

Gabriele Glang, is a German-American bilingual poet and artist Gabriele Glang has been living in a small village on the Swabian Alb in southern Germany for nearly three decades. In 2017 Klöpfer & Meyer Verlag published her German poetry debut, *"Göttertage,"* fictional monologues of German Expressionist painter Paula Modersohn-Becker. A screenwriter and freelance translator in the film sector, Glang teaches creative writing in English at the University of Applied Sciences at Esslingen. www.gabrieleglang.de

William Greenway's *Selected Poems* is from FutureCycle Press and his newest and twelfth collection is *The Accidental Garden* from Word Press. His collections, *Everywhere at Once* and *Ascending Order* (both from University of Akron Press Poetry Series) won Poetry Book of the Year Awards from the Ohio Library Association. His poems have appeared in *American Poetry Review, Poetry, Missouri Review, Southern Review, Georgia Review, Southern Poetry Review, Prairie Schooner, Poetry Northwest,* and *Shenandoah.* He has won numerous awards including Georgia Author of the Year. He is Distinguished Professor of English Emeritus at Youngstown State University and lives in Ephrata, Pennsylvania.

John Grey is an Australian poet, US resident in Rhode Island. Recently published in *Midwest Quarterly, Poetry East* and *North Dakota Quarterly* with work upcoming in *South Florida Poetry Journal, Hawaii Review* and the *Dunes Review.*

An editor, writer, and poet, **Charles Grosel** lives in Arizona. He has published stories in *Western Humanities Review, Red Cedar Review, Water-Stone,* and *The MacGuffin* as well as poems in *Tipton Poetry Review, Slate, The Threepenny Review, Poet Lore,* and *Harpur Palate,* among others. To pay the bills, Charles owns the communications firm, *Write for Success.*

Andrew Hamilton graduated from Saint Mary's College of California with his MFA. His work has appeared in The Saturday Evening Post's Great American Fiction Contest, Blue Fifth Review, BlazeVOX, The Rush, Glassworks, Reed Magazine, Crack the Spine, and Yes Poetry with new poems forthcoming in The Main Street Rag, Dream Pop Journal, and Maudlin House. He lives near Seattle where he teaches English and History at Brightmont Academy while providing service work for the recovery community.

Rehanul Hoque, born in the village of Majkhuria in Bangladesh, studied M.A in English literature and pursued an MSc in International Development from a UK University. He is a bilingual poet and started writing poems at an early age. Though he has an interest in different forms of literature, his first and foremost love is poetry. Rehanul lives in Bangladesh.

Gil Hoy is a Boston poet and semi-retired trial lawyer studying poetry at Boston University through its Evergreen program. Hoy previously received a B.A. in Philosophy and Political Science from Boston University, an M.A. in Government from Georgetown University, and a J.D. from the University of Virginia School of Law. He served as a Brookline, Massachusetts Selectman for four terms. Hoy's poetry has appeared in *Chiron Review, The New Verse News, Ariel Chart, Social Justice Poetry, The Potomac, The Penmen Review* and elsewhere.

Scott T. Hutchison is a New Hampshire poet. Previous work has appeared in *The Georgia Review* and *The Southern Review*. Poems are forthcoming in *Appalachian Heritage, Concho River Review, Louisiana Literature, The Naugatuck River Review, Red Dirt Forum, Steam Ticket* and *Tar River Poetry*. A new book of poetry, *Moonshine Narratives*, is available from Main Street Rag Publishing.

James Croal Jackson has a chapbook, *The Frayed Edge of Memory* (Writing Knights Press, 2017), and poems in *Pacifica, indefinite space*, and *Philosophical Idiot*. He edits *The Mantle*. Currently, he works in the film industry in Pittsburgh. jimjakk.com

Sean Kelbley lives on a farm in southeastern Ohio, in a house he and his husband built. He works as an elementary school counselor. Sean's poetry has been recognized in contests at *Midwest Review, Still: The Journal, Up North Lit, the Yuki Teikei Haiku Society*, and has appeared online and/or in print at *Crab Creek Review, One, Rattle, Rise Up Review* (2017 Best of the Net nomination), and other wonderful places.

Erren Geraud Kelly's work has appeared in numerous publications in print and online in various literary journals and magazines throughout the United States, Canada and Europe. Mr. Kelly is the author of the book Disturbing The Peace, on Night Ballet Press. Erren received his BA in English – Creative Writing from Louisiana State University in Baton Rouge. Kelly lives in Los Angeles.

Helga Kidder lives in the Tennessee hills with her husband and dog. She was awarded an MFA from Vermont College and am co-founder of the Chattanooga Writers Guild. Her poems have been published in *Haight Ashbury Literary Journal, Poetry South, Slipstream*, and in *Carrying the Branch: Poets in Search of Peace* anthology. Helga has three poetry books: *Wild Plums, Luckier than the Stars*, and *Blackberry Winter*.

Steve Klepetar lives in the Berkshires in Massachusetts. His work has received several nominations for Best of the Net and the Pushcart Prize. The most recent of his fourteen collections include *A Landscape in Hell,Why Glass Shatters*, and *The Coffee Drinker's Son*.

Edward Lee poetry, short stories, non-fiction and photography have been published in magazines in Ireland, England and America, including *The Stinging Fly, Skylight 47, Acumen* and *Smiths Knoll*. Edward lives in Ireland. His debut poetry collection *Playing Poohsticks On Ha'Penny Bridge* was published in 2010. He is currently working towards a second collection. He also makes musical noise under the names *Ayahuasca Collective, Lewis Milne, Orson Carroll, Blinded Architect, Lego Figures Fighting*, and *Pale Blond Boy*. His Facebook page can be found at www.facebook.com/edwardleewriter.

Bruce Levine, a 2019 Pushcart Prize Poetry Nominee, has spent his life as a writer of fiction and poetry and as a music and theatre professional. His literary catalogue includes four novels, short stories, humorous sketches, flash fiction, poetry, essays, articles and a screenplay. Nearly 150 of his works are published in over 25 on-line journals including *Ariel Chart, Friday Flash Fiction, Literally Stories*; over 30 print books including *Poetry Quarterly, Haiku Journal, Dual Coast Magazine*, and his shows have been produced in New York and around the country. His 7 eBooks are available from Amazon.com. His work is dedicated to the loving memory of his late wife, Lydia Franklin. He lives in New York with his dog, Daisy. Visit him at www.brucelevine.com.

Paul Lojeski was born and raised in Lakewood, Ohio. He attended Oberlin College. His poetry has appeared online and in print. He lives in Port Jefferson, New York.

A retired educator living in a small town in Eastern Oregon, **Jack E. Lorts** has appeared extensively, if infrequently, over the past 40+ years in such magazines as *Arizona Quarterly, Kansas Quarterly, English Journal, Agnostic Lobster* and *Fishtrap,* among others. Author of three chapbooks, *The Daughter Poems & Others...* and *The Meeting-Place of Words,* published by Pudding House, and *Dear Gilbert Sorrentino & Other Poems* from Finishing Line Press. Uttered Chaos Press of Eugene, Oregon recently published his *The Love Songs of Ephram Pratt.* Active in local and state Democratic politics, he served as Mayor of Fossil, Oregon for many years; currently lives in The Dalles, Oregon.

Richard Luftig is a former professor of educational psychology and special education at Miami University in Ohio now residing in California. His poems and stories have appeared in numerous literary journals in the United States (INCLUDING *TIPTON POETRY JOURNAL* and internationally in Canada, Australia, Europe, and Asia. Two of his poems recently appeared in *Realms of the Mothers: The First Decade of Dos Madres Press.* His latest book of poems is available from *Unsolicited Press in 2019.* His webpage and blog may be found at richardluftig.com

Marianne Lyon has been a music teacher for 43 years. After teaching in Hong Kong, she returned to the Napa Valley and has been published in various literary magazines and reviews including *Ravens Perch, TWJM Magazine, Earth Daughters* and *Indiana Voice Journal.* She was nominated for the *Pushcart Prize* in 2017. She is a member of the *California Writers Club* and an Adjunct Professor at Touro University in California.

A native of Norfolk, Virginia, **Alex MacConochie** currently lives and writes in Somerville, Massachusetts. His poems appear in *Tar River Poetry, The Summerset Review, Louisiana Literature, Constellations,* and elsewhere.

Sem Megson's poetry and plays have been published and produced in the United States, the United Kingdom, and Canada. Sem lives in Toronto. For more information, visit semmegson.com.

Karla Linn Merrifield, a nine-time Pushcart Prize nominee and National Park Artist-in-Residence, has had 700+ poems appear in dozens of journals and anthologies. She has 14 books to her credit. Following her 2018 *Psyche's Scroll* (Poetry Box Select) is the newly released full-length book *Athabaskan Fractal: Poems of the Far North from Cirque Press. Her Godwit: Poems of Canada* (FootHills Publishing) received the Eiseman Award for Poetry. She now lives in Florida and is a frequent contributor to *The Songs of Eretz Poetry Review,* and assistant editor and poetry book reviewer Emerita for *The Centrifugal Eye..*

Frank Modica is a retired public school teacher in Urbana, Illinois. He taught students with special needs for 34 years. Since his retirement he volunteers with a number of arts and social service organizations in his community. His work has appeared in *Spindrift Literary Arts Journal, Slab, Heyday Magazine, Cacti Fur Magazine, The Tishman Review, Crab Fat Literary Magazine,* and *Black Heart Magazine.*

Keith Moul has written poems and taken photos for more than 50 years, his work appearing in magazines widely. His chapbook, *The Journal*, was recently accepted by Duck Lake Chaps for issuance in early 2020. This is his ninth chap or book published. These poems follow the voices of pioneers over wide plains of the U.S. Keith Moul has lived among these voices, owes them fealty because people survive the plains under the most adverse conditions. He has come to appreciate the knack to this bravery, now much later in his life.

Thomas Osatchoff, together with family, is building a self-sustaining home near a waterfall in The Philippines. Recent poems have appeared in *Breakwater Review, FOLIO, HCE Review*, and elsewhere.

Carl "Papa" Palmer of Old Mill Road in Ridgeway, Virginia, lives in University Place, Washington. He is retired from the military and Federal Aviation Administration (FAA) enjoying life now as "Papa" to his grand descendants and being a Franciscan Hospice volunteer. Carl is a *Pushcart Prize* and *Micro Award* nominee.

Chris Pellizzari is a graduate of the University of Illinois at Urbana-Champaign. His work has appeared in numerous literary magazines, including *COUNTERCLOCK, Schuylkill Valley Journal, Open: Journal of Arts & Letters,* and *Allegro Poetry Magazine.* He is a member of *The Society of Midland Authors* and is assistant editor at *The Awakenings Review.* Chris lives in Illinois.

Roger Pfingston is the recipient of two PEN Syndicated Fiction Awards and a poetry fellowship from the National Endowment for the Arts. He lives in Bloomington, Indiana and is the author of *Something Iridescent*, a collection of poetry and fiction, as well as four chapbooks: *Earthbound, Singing to the Garden,* and *A Day Marked for Telling* and *What's Given.* He has poems in *I-70 Review, U.S. 1 Worksheets, Plainsongs, Innisfree Poetry Journal, American Journal of Poetry,* and *Poet Lore.*

Robin Ray, formerly of *Trinidad & Tobago*, resides in Port Townsend, Washington. His works have appeared at *Red Fez, Scarlet Leaf Review, Aphelion, Spark, Neologism Poetry Journal*, and elsewhere.

Patrick T. Reardon is the author of eight books, including the poetry collection *Requiem for David* and *Faith Stripped to Its Essence*, a literary-religious analysis of Shusaku Endo's novel *Silence*. Reardon, who worked as a Chicago Tribune reporter for 32 years, has published essays and book reviews widely in such publications as the Tribune, Chicago Sun-Times, Crain's Chicago Business, National Catholic Reporter and U.S. Catholic. His poems, nominated twice for a Pushcart Prize, have appeared throughout the U.S. as well as in Paris and India. His novella *Babe* was short-listed by Stewart O'Nan for the annual Faulkner-Wisdom Contest.

Timothy Robbins has been teaching English as a Second Language for 28 years. He has been a regular contributor to *Hanging Loose* since 1980. His poems have appeared in *Main Street Rag, Off The Coast, Bayou Magazine, Slant, Tipton Poetry Journal, Cholla Needles* and many others. He has published three volumes of poetry: *Three New Poets (Hanging Loose Press), Denny's Arbor Vitae (Adelaide Books)* and *Carrying Bodies (Main Street Rag Press).* He lives in Wisconsin with his husband of 21 years.

John Timothy Robinson is a mainstream poet of the expressive image and inwardness from the Kanawha Valley in Mason County, West Virginia. His poetics was developed in the tradition of James Wright, Rita Dove, Donald Hall, Marvin Bell, Maxine Kumin, WS Merwin, Tess Gallagher and Robert Bly among many others. John's works have appeared in ninety-nine journals throughout the United States, Canada, the United Kingdom and India. He is also a published printmaker with eighty-two art images and photographs appearing in journals, electronic and print in the United States, Italy and Ireland.

Dave Seter is a civil engineer and poet. Originally from Chicago, he currently lives in Sonoma County, California. His poetry and critical works have recently appeared in *Paterson Literary Review, Evansville Review, Palaver, Confluence,* and other journals. He received his undergraduate degree from Princeton University and his graduate degree from Dominican University of California, where he studied ecopoetics. His poetry chapbook *Night Duty* was published in 2010 by *Main Street Rag Publishing Company.*

Michael Shepley is a writer/researcher in Sacramento, California. His poems appeared in print in *California Quarterly, Muse International (India), Seems, Xanadu* and *DM du Jour.*

Canadian poet, fiction writer, and playwright **J. J. Steinfeld** lives on Prince Edward Island, where he is patiently waiting for Godot's arrival and a phone call from Kafka. While waiting, he has published 19 books, including *Absurdity, Woe Is Me, Glory Be* (Guernica Editions, 2017), and *A Visit to the Kafka Café* (Ekstasis Editions, 2018). His short stories and poems have appeared in numerous periodicals and anthologies internationally, and over 50 of his one-act plays and a handful of full-length plays have been performed in Canada and the United States.

Leah Stenson lives in Oregon and is the author of two chapbooks, *Heavenly Body* and *The Turquoise Bee and Other Love Poems* (Finishing Line Press: 2011 and 2014, respectively); a regional editor of *Alive at the Center: Contemporary Poems from the Pacific Northwest* (Ooligan Press, 2013) and co-editor of *Reverberations from Fukushima* (Inkwater Press, 2014) which was awarded finalist status in the category of Social Change in the USA Best Book Awards and first place for Poetry in the Pacific Rim Book Festival.. Her full-length book of poetry *Everywhere I Find Myself* was published by Turning Point in December 2017. She serves on the board of Tavern Books. Please see www.leahstenson.com.

Ziaeddin Torabi is an Iranian-American poet living in Sacramento who has published more than 30 books in different areas, including poetry, translation, criticism, and review. From 1988-1998, he was the head of the Tehran Municipal Cultural Center, and from 1999-2009, he taught Literature at the University of Applied Sciences and Technology in Tehran. He has won many literary awards, including the 2010 Iran Annual Book Prize for his poetry collection, *Face To Face with Dreams*, published in English translation by *Ad Lumen Press.*

John Tustin began writing poetry after in February 2008 after a ten year hiatus and finally became brave enough to submit to magazines in April of 2009. In August of that year received his first acceptance from Poem and from *Straylight* that December. Since then his poetry has appeared in well over 100 literary journals, online and in print. fritzware.com/johntustinpoetry contains links to his published poetry online.

Gene Twaronite a Tucson poet and the author of seven books, including two short story collections and two juvenile fantasy novels. His first book of poetry *Trash Picker on Mars* was published by Kelsay Books, and was the winner of the 2017 New Mexico/Arizona Book Award for Arizona poetry. His newest collection is *The Museum of Unwearable Shoes*.

Iain Twiddy studied literature at university and lived for several years in northern Japan. He has poems published or forthcoming in *Salamander, Quiddity, The Blue Mountain Review, The Dalhousie Review, Flyway* and elsewhere.

Keith Welch lives in Bloomington, Indiana where he works at the Indiana University Herman B Wells library. He has poems published in T*he Tipton Poetry Journal, Open: Journal of Arts & Letters, Dime Show Review, and Literary Orphans*, among others. He enjoys complicated board games, baking, talking to his cat, Alice, and meeting other poets. His website is keithwelchpoetry.com

Marne Wilson lives in Parkersburg, West Virginia. Her poems have recently appeared in *Whale Road Review* and *Hobart* and are forthcoming in *Gargoyle* and *Crab Orchard Review*. She is the author of two chapbooks, *The Bovine Daycare Center (Finishing Line, 2015)* and *As Lovers Always Do (Etchings Press, 2019)*.

Marie Gray Wise's work has appeared in *U.S. 1 Worksheets, The Café Review, Naugatuck River Review, Grey Sparrow Journal, The Paterson Literary Review,* and *English Journal.*

CPSIA information can be obtained
at www.ICGtesting.com
Printed in the USA
LVHW110508041119
636231LV00001B/50/P